The Electric Knife Way to Better Carving

The Electric Knife Way to

# BETTER CARVING

FOR HIM AND HER... FOR EVERY DAY... EVERY MENU... EVERY COOK

# Edited by Betty Sullivan

*Designed and Illustrated by Roland Rodegast*     *Photographs by Food Photographers, Inc., New York*

ALL RECIPES HAVE BEEN TESTED IN THE HAMILTON BEACH KITCHENS AT RACINE, WISCONSIN.

FIRST EDITION     FIRST PRINTING

# Contents

# Introduction

## FOR EVERY DAY...EVERY MENU...EVERY COOK

THE ELECTRIC KNIFE WAY TO BETTER CARVING is for him and for her. It's a step-by-step carving manual as well as an all-occasion recipe-menu book. The pages are brimful of culinary ideas that run the gamut from savory appetizers to taste-tempting desserts. And, they're all inspired by the ease and convenience of the electric knife.

The recipes allow for the maximum use of this remarkable home appliance which shares the same versatility as your electric mixer or blender. When first marketed, the electric knife was considered just another appliance, but its true value in preparing as well as serving different types of foods was soon recognized and acclaimed.

Breakfast, lunch or dinner—perfect cutting insures the full taste and texture of all your foods. Raw and cooked meats can be trimmed, cubed or thinly sliced more easily and efficiently for casseroles or kabobs. Vegetables and fruits can be diced, sliced, cubed or halved without tearing or bruising. Breads, cakes, cooky dough and even tortes with sumptuous fillings can be perfectly and evenly sliced. The electric knife makes all foods fresher looking, more attractive and more appetizing.

And the man of the house has not been forgotten. He'll find easy-to-follow carving instructions and diagrams for popular cuts of pork, lamb, beef, ham and poultry. These basic how-to's will add to the proficiency of his carving technique. Similarly, if the hostess prefers to serve the meat already sliced, she, too, can masterfully carve any cut of meat.

Whether you're a gourmet cook, "career girl," new bride or mother of four, all of the menus have been planned with you in mind. You'll find exciting meals for every day of the week, buffet-style dinners, special menus for entertaining, new ideas for holiday feasts and backyard barbecues. Of course, the traditional favorites have been included, but they're dressed up with new and different "serve-with" ideas or colorful garnishes. In addition, the buffet, entertaining and holiday menus include wine suggestions for the host or hostess who's hesitant about which wines to serve

with what foods. *And,* the menus we suggest are really just the beginning. Interchange the recipes and adapt the menus to suit your individual needs as well as your personal tastes and preferences.

Plan your own menus, both formal and informal, for each and any of the many special occasions throughout the year—birthdays, anniversaries, luncheons, dinners at the beach or on the patio. Perhaps you've invited some friends for tea and bridge or after-dinner dessert and coffee. One of our many dessert recipes will be just perfect for occasions such as these.

If your next party or perhaps a holiday celebration calls for an extra note of gaiety, why not decorate? Let the menus spark your imagination or choose a seasonal theme, and make decorations just as simple or elaborate as you wish. Several menus even include foreign-inspired foods (such as Sukiyaki and Polynesian Pork) which lend themselves so readily to an international motif. Fruits, vegetables, flowers, candles, unusual china, glassware, travel posters or colorful paper ornaments offer unlimited possibilities. A color scheme always makes special occasions a bit more festive. Especially for buffet service, you can mix and match the patterns and colors of your china, linens and even glassware. Unusual serving pieces will enhance your foods as well as your table. A chafing dish or casserole with a candle warmer not only adds a touch of glamor but keeps foods hot and appetizing. If you're serving fresh fruits for dessert, arrange them before dinner and use as a centerpiece. Many of the colorful photographs throughout the book provide a multitude of other decorating and serving ideas. Have fun and give your imagination free rein!

*And now,* turn the pages and discover for yourself that THE ELECTRIC KNIFE WAY TO BETTER CARVING is truly for every day, every menu and every cook. It's a boon for anyone who aspires to be a "chef extraordinaire."

*Betty Sullivan*

# How to Assemble, Use and Care for an Electric Knife

• Before using your electric knife for the first time, separate the blades, and wash off any light oil coating with a soap-filled steel wool pad. This will insure cleanliness and smoother operation.

• The blades are extremely sharp. Always handle them by the side opposite the serrated cutting edge or by the plastic guards, never by the blade edges. Follow the manufacturer's instructions for assembling your knife unit.

• The back and forth action of the matched pair of blades does all the work. There's no need whatever to "saw." Simply guide the knife blade in its cutting operation.

• If the blades of your electric knife rotate for horizontal cutting, push the turret in and turn the blade 90°. The knife motor unit and handle remain in the normal upright position. These units are specially adapted for either a right- or left-handed person. A right-handed person rotates the blade clockwise, while a left-handed person inserts the blades upside down and also turns them clockwise.

• Always disconnect the cord from electric outlet or lock unit in off position when knife is not in use or before removing blades.

• After using the knife, remove blades and slip them apart for easy cleaning. Wash blades in hot soapy water as you would any fine cutlery; rinse and dry thoroughly. Wipe motor unit with a clean damp cloth, if necessary, and dry. Never immerse motor unit in water.

• Most blades come in a plastic sleeve which should be used for storage. This sleeve will protect the blades and make blade handling safer. The entire knife unit may be stored in its tray or drawer space—just be sure it's in a handy ready-to-use location.

• Use a wooden cutting surface whenever possible. This will protect the blades, especially when you're cutting vertically.

• When carving meats, cut down to and around any bones—never attempt to cut through them.

• The electric knife blades are not designed to cut solid frozen foods.

• Blades should not need sharpening if they are given proper care. However, if the blades become dull, do not try to sharpen them yourself. Return them to the manufacturer's authorized service center.

# Knife-wise Ways with...
# VEGETABLES

Artichokes
Asparagus
Beets
Broccoli
Cabbage
Carrots
Cauliflower
Celery
Cucumber
Eggplant
Green and red peppers
Leeks
Lettuce
Onions
Potatoes
Small acorn squash
Tomatoes
Turnips
Zucchini

## Appetizers

• Cut celery strips lengthwise and serve plain or stuffed with cheese.

• Marinate cucumber or beet and onion slices in French or garlic dressing.

• Serve cucumber, carrot and celery strips with sour cream or favorite dip.

• Cut leeks in one-inch pieces and parboil. Cut pieces in half and stuff with caviar, chopped egg or horseradish.

• Garnish tomato slices with anchovy and green pepper strips; season with pepper, oil and vinegar.

## Garnishes

• Serve coleslaw garnished with green pepper strips or rings.

• Dip tomato slices or wedges in finely chopped parsley or chives.

• Dip asparagus tips in white sauce or sour cream.

• Sauté tomato slices, or sprinkle tomato halves with bread crumbs and shredded cheese; broil.

• For texture contrast, garnish vegetable dishes with toasted bread cubes. Stack 3 or 4 slices of bread; remove crusts and cube for croutons.

## Vegetable Dishes

• Dice cooked artichoke hearts and serve with a white cream sauce.

• Arrange cooked asparagus in a baking dish; cover the tips with grated cheese and bread crumbs. Cover dish with foil and bake in oven until cheese melts.

• Serve cooked asparagus tips on toast triangles with Hollandaise sauce.

• Simmer turnip, celery, carrot, parsnip slices and many other vegetables in bouillon.

• Sauté onion slices in butter and serve with mixture of sour cream and caraway seeds.

## Salads

• Serve artichoke hearts, tomato, green pepper and hard-cooked egg slices with French dressing.

• Dice cooked sweet potatoes and tomatoes. Mix with garlic mayonnaise and serve on lettuce with strips of chicken or croutons.

• Top shredded lettuce with cooked string beans and peas, tomato wedges and quartered hard-cooked eggs. Serve with mayonnaise seasoned with Worcestershire sauce.

• Try carrot strips, mushrooms, cooked asparagus spears and tomato aspic cubes with French dressing.

# Knife-wise Ways with...
# MEATS

Trim, slice, cube, bone or cut as desired all raw and cooked meats. (Raw meats are easier to cut if partially frozen.)

### Appetizers

• Place thin slices of fried ham on toast squares; top with a mushroom and sprinkle with parsley or spread with pickle relish. Serve hot as hors d'oeuvres.

• Place thin slices of tongue on toast squares and spread with mustard butter.

• Top cubes of bologna, salami and ham loaf with olive or small pickle and skewer with toothpick.

• Spread thin slices of bologna or salami with cream cheese and roll into a cornucopia.

• Spread bologna slices with horse-radish and cream cheese; place on top of each other and cut into triangles.

• Spread thin slices of tongue or beef with cream cheese flavored with Worcestershire sauce; roll and fasten with toothpick.

### Garnishes

• Cut cold cooked meats in julienne strips and garnish vegetables and salads.

• Sauté thin slices of tongue in butter and fill with chopped mushrooms. Roll and tie each slice with red pimiento strip; fasten with toothpick.

• Fry thin slices of ham and wrap around large mushrooms.

### Salads

• Toss strips of cooked beef, potatoes and asparagus tips with mayonnaise.

• Serve strips of cooked tongue, ham and chicken with sliced artichoke hearts and French dressing.

• Place strips of cold tongue, sliced celery and beets on shredded lettuce with mayonnaise.

• Dice cold beef, apples, pineapple and orange sections; serve with French dressing.

• Marinate shredded cabbage in French dressing; cover with strips of cold beef, tongue or ham and garnish with green pepper rings.

• Serve diced ham, tomato wedges and cold string beans with sour cream dressing.

• Cut ham in strips and dice cooked potatoes; mix with cooked lima beans, chopped filberts and mayonnaise.

### Leftover Meat Ideas

• Dice leftover corned beef, lamb or roast beef and mix with your choice of the following for a flavorful hash: diced cooked potatoes, chopped onions, green or red peppers, bread crumbs, grated cheese, egg yolk, tomato paste or chopped tomatoes.

• Dip tongue slices in egg and bread crumbs; deep fry.

• For curries or casseroles, dice, cube or cut leftover meat into strips.

• Make sandwiches with leftover ham, turkey, roast beef or lamb. Stack several sandwiches and cut in half or quarter.

# Knife-wise Ways with...
# FRUITS AND CHEESES

Apples
Grapefruit
Lemons
Limes
Melons
Oranges
Pears
Pineapple
Rhubarb

Bel Paese
Blue
Brie
Cheddar
Edam or Gouda
Fontina
Gorgonzola
Gruyère
Mozzarella
Muenster
Port du Salut
Provalone
Romano
Roquefort
Swiss

### Appetizers
• Fill half a cantaloupe or small honeydew melon with berries.
• Serve melon cubes sprinkled with a few tablespoons sherry or port, or cover them with equal parts of melted mint jelly and ginger ale blended together.
• Place small cubes of cheese in the centers of pear halves and bake until cheese melts.
• Fill apple rings with Roquefort cheese or chicken salad.
• Pare small melon wedges and serve with thin slices of ham.
• Combine chilled cooked rhubarb with berries.

• Sprinkle melon strips, pineapple chunks and other fruits with finely chopped mint and serve with your favorite cheese dip or sour cream.
• Roll cheese straws in finely chopped nuts.
• Top cheese cubes with a small pickle or olive and skewer with toothpick.

### Garnishes
• Fill orange shells with cranberry sauce, mint or apple jelly; fill lemon shells with tartare sauce or horseradish.
• Place spoonfuls of jelly on orange or lemon slices.
• Sauté pineapple slices in butter and serve garnished with jelly or a maraschino cherry.
• Serve fried apple rings with veal or pork.
• Simmer citrus fruit slices in wine or sauté in butter.
• Garnish meats with slices of spiced fruits.
• Fill apple rings or pear halves with chopped mushrooms and nuts.
• Top cereals with sliced fresh fruit, or add diced apples or other fruit to pancake batter.
• Slice Italian or French bread and place slice of cheddar cheese in each slit before heating.

### Salads
• Fill pear or peach halves with Roquefort, cream cheese or cottage cheese mixed with chopped chives; serve on shredded lettuce.

• Poach apple slices in sugar syrup. Serve on bed of crisp lettuce and top with mayonnaise or whipped cream; sprinkle with shredded coconut.
• Serve sliced tomatoes and pineapple on lettuce with sour cream dressing.
• Top a pineapple slice with coleslaw, Waldorf salad or fruited gelatin.

### Desserts
• Sprinkle pear or peach halves with sugar and bake in fruit juice until hot.
• Fill orange shells with sherbet or ice cream. Serve topped with meringue or whipped cream.
• Poach apple or pear slices in wine or sugar syrup; top with sweetened whipped cream and sprinkle with crushed macaroons or top with vanilla ice cream and crushed berries.
• Cut up fruits, such as rhubarb, for pie filling.
• Serve slices or wedges of melon à la mode or with berries.
• Assorted fresh fruits and cheeses or a fruit compote are often the perfect dessert.
• Soak melon cubes, orange slices or other fruits in kirsch and serve with whipped cream, if desired.
• Place a slice of ice cream on a cake slice; top with a pear half, fruit syrup or chocolate sauce.
• Fill pear or peach halves with jelly and top with vanilla flavored whipped cream.

# Knife-wise Ways with...
# CAKES, COOKIES AND ICE CREAM DESSERTS

Angel food cake
Fruitcake
Layer cake
Meringues
Pound cake
Shortcake
Sponge cake
Tortes
Refrigerated cooky dough
Bricks of ice cream
Ice cream molds

• Slice bricks of ice cream and serve, or wrap individually and re-freeze. Cut thin slices of ice cream and pound cake; make sandwiches and serve with fruit topping or hot sauce.

• Cut refrigerated cooky dough into uniform slices.

• Slice glazed or fruit topped coffee cakes or crumb cakes.

• Cut sponge or angel food cake into three or four layers. Fill between layers and frost top of cake with flavored whipped cream. Garnish cake with chopped maraschino cherries, crushed macaroons or finely chopped nuts.

• Soak sponge or pound cake cubes or strips in fruit liqueur or sugar syrup. Combine cake mixture with softened ice cream; place in mold and freeze. Slice and serve with whipped cream, if desired.

• Cut meringue into slices. Put two slices together with butter cream filling and top with caramelized sugar.

• Soak slices of pound cake in rum and serve topped with ice cream, fresh fruit or chocolate sauce.

• Cut sponge, layer or angel food cake into six slices and sprinkle each slice with Madeira wine. Alternately spread slices with apricot jam and raspberry jelly; top with meringue and brown slices in the oven.

• Cut pound cake into bite-sized cubes and frost with flavored icings.

# Car

**Good food** is always enjoyable but what makes it good? Four basic elements—menu planning, food preparation, serving *and* carving—make our daily meals pleasurable. All four involve practice and a certain amount of skill, but the importance of carving is too often overlooked. Planning and preparation set the stage, but the presentation begins with carving. Correct carving will capture the full taste and texture of your foods. The natural juices will not escape to the serving platter but will be retained in the meat. Whatever the type of meat, it will be more succulent and flavorful if properly carved. Generous cuts of roast beef, thin delicate slices of turkey or pork not only mean greater dining pleasure but also insure more attractive individual plates.

The art of carving in itself should be a great appetite stimulator. We have all watched the well-meaning efforts of a host or hostess who intends to serve generous portions but ends up with ragged shreds and small, uneven slices. Or we have witnessed the precise, surgical endeavors of the home-variety maitre d' who takes so long carving that the food is cold by the time it's served. Both these extremes can now be a thing of the past. The electric knife offers everyone —man or woman—the opportunity to be a master in the art of carving. Heretofore, the would-be carver's Waterloo was lack of control in manipulating the knife blade. However, an•electric knife offers efficiency and convenience—all the carver has to do is guide the knife in its carving or slicing operation. Once this effortless approach is followed, the carving struggle is over forever—no more mutilated poultry, hacked roasts or shredded fish.

With a few basic rules and carving tips, the specific techniques become a simple, easy procedure that anyone can learn. As is true of any skill, common sense should always prevail.

One of the first rules for good carving is an understanding of the carving tools. Learn what your electric knife can do and how to use it in the easiest, most efficient way. If the blades of your knife rotate, you can more comfortably and accurately carve any meat that requires horizontal cutting, and there is no need to change your natural grip of the knife handle. Holding the knife comfortably for either vertical or horizontal cutting will build your confidence, so that you will be able to carve any type of meat, poultry or fish.

●

A good two-tined carving fork, preferably with a guard, is a must not only for holding the meat securely on the carving surface but also for serving.

●

Spoons for serving stuffing, garnishes and the natural meat juices should be within easy reach.

●

To insure that each serving is hot when eaten, it's always advisable to heat the platter on which the meat will be carved. Also, when carving vertically, it's wise to protect both the blade and your porcelain or metal platters by carving on a wooden cutting board, or if possible, use a platter with a wooden insert.

●

Essential to a good carving technique is allowing the meat or poultry to stand for at least ten to fifteen minutes after it has been placed on the heated platter. This permits the meat to firm up and thus makes carving much easier. Smooth, uniform cuts can be made with facility, and the appearance as well as the flavor of the meat is enhanced.

# ving

Except for rolled or crown roasts, be sure all thread, cord or skewers have been removed prior to carving.

•

Good carving requires plenty of elbowroom. Be sure candlesticks, glasses, salt and pepper shakers and the centerpiece will not be in your way while carving.

•

Another helpful hint is to have an auxiliary heated platter close at hand to provide a resting place for garnishes, slices of a large roast or for bones. This will also allow a clear area for carving.

•

To carve sitting down or standing up is a decision for the carver and depends on which position is more comfortable. Naturally, you must stand to carve a standing rib roast that's in the upright position. A boneless cut of meat, such as a cushion lamb shoulder, is on a lower level and may be more comfortably carved if you're sitting down. On the other hand, one wouldn't consider sitting down to carve a large roast turkey because of its height and drama.

•

Just before carving, stop for a moment and ask yourself—how many servings are needed? Use your best judgment and put an end to huge or skimpy portions. And, remember, to protect the full flavor of the meat and retain the heat, carve only one side of the roast or fowl at a time, and carve only as much as you'll need.

**Correct carving** certainly does not require a knowledge of animal anatomy, but it is essential for the carver to know the location of the bones, muscles and tendons as well as the grain of the specific cut to be carved. For that reason, diagrams and specific carving directions for the most popular cuts of meat have been included here. These how-to's of carving outline procedures and techniques that will insure perfect texture and perfect taste. Therefore, it is wise to follow these instructions until they become habit.

With ease and confidence you will be able to master the carving of any cut of meat—the intricacies of a roast loin of pork or the slicing of a beef brisket. Indulge your family and friends in custom-made servings and greater dining pleasure. And remember, no matter what type of meat you're serving it will always be more succulent and flavorful when properly carved.

Enjoy yourself.
Bon appétit!

17

## Standing Rib Roast

When purchasing roast, ask butcher to separate the backbone from the ribs and to remove the short ribs. Carving will be much easier with the backbone removed and only the rib bones remaining.

Place roast on a heated serving platter. The larger cut surface should face down and the rib side should be to your left. (If your electric knife has an adjustable blade, rotate for horizontal carving.)

Insert carving fork with guard securely between the two top ribs. Starting at the far right outside edge, slice across the grain (or face of roast) toward rib side. *See first diagram.* Slice several servings approximately ¼ inch thick.

(Return adjustable blade to vertical carving position.) To release each slice, cut along full length of rib bone with knife. *See second diagram.*

Lift each slice as it is cut on the knife blade, steadying it with fork, and place on side of platter. (Use another hot platter if meat platter is not large enough to hold slices.) *See third diagram.*

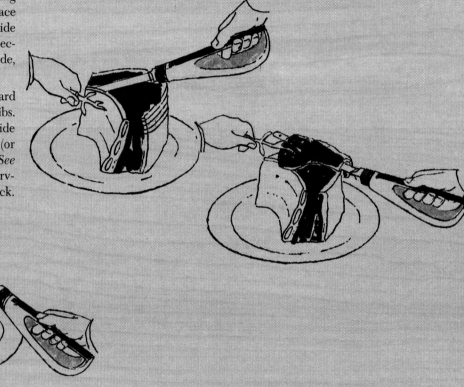

## Rolled Rib Roast

Place roast on a heated serving platter. The larger cut surface should face down. (If your electric knife has an adjustable blade, rotate for horizontal carving.)

Insert carving fork with guard securely in the left side of roast 2 or 3 inches below the top. Cut and remove each cord only as it is reached while carving. (Do not cut strings prior to carving or the roast will fall apart.)

Starting at the far right side, slice across the grain (or face of roast) toward the fork. *See first diagram.* Carve slices approximately ¼ inch thick.

Lift each slice as it is cut on the knife blade, steadying it with fork, and place on side of platter. (Use another hot platter if meat platter is not large enough to hold slices.) *See second diagram.*

18

## Porterhouse Steak

Unlike any other cut of beef, steak is carved *with* the grain because of the tenderness and short fibers of the meat. Place steak on cutting board or platter with a wooden insert. The bone should be to your right.

Insert carving fork securely in the left portion of steak and cut as closely as possible around the T-shaped bone. *See first diagram.* Remove bone and set aside.

With fork still inserted in the left side, cut from top to bottom across the full width of steak. *See second diagram.*

Continue carving slices about an inch wide across meat. If you carve in this manner, each slice will contain part of the tenderloin and part of the large muscle. Cut the tail or flank end in the same manner if additional servings are needed. *See third diagram.*

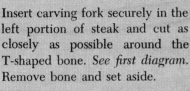

## Blade Pot Roast

This cut of beef contains part of one rib and a piece of the blade-bone. Usually, the bones can be easily removed immediately after cooking. Place pot roast on cutting board or platter with a wooden insert.

Insert carving fork securely in the left side of meat. The surface of the roast is divided into several meaty sections (or muscles). Separate the first section by cutting between two muscles as shown (and then along the bone if it was not removed before serving). *See first diagram.*

Turn section and hold with fork so the grain is running parallel to the carving surface. This will allow you to cut across the grain of the meat. *See second diagram.*

Carve slices ¼ to ½ inch thick. *See third diagram.* Continue to separate and carve each meat section in the same manner.

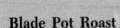

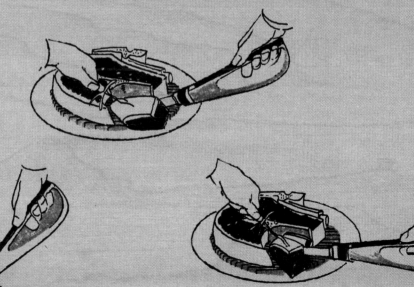

## Baked Whole Ham

Place ham on a heated serving platter. The fat side should face up and the shank end and bone should be to your right.

Insert carving fork in large part (or butt) to steady ham. Cut two or three thin slices parallel to the length of ham from the thin side. (The thin side will face you if ham is a left leg or face away from you if ham is a right leg.) *See first diagram.*

Rest ham on the thin cut side where first slices were made. The shank bone is now pointing up. Holding ham firmly with fork, cut a small wedge about 6 inches in from the shank end. Remove wedge. *See second diagram.* This allows for easier carving and releasing of the slices.

Starting at wedge, continue to carve thin vertical slices straight down almost to the leg bone. (If your electric knife has an adjustable blade, rotate for horizontal carving.) With fork still in meat, start at the shank end and run knife along leg bone at right angles to the slices. This will release already carved slices. *See third diagram.* Additional servings may be carved by placing ham in original position and slicing at right angles to the bone.

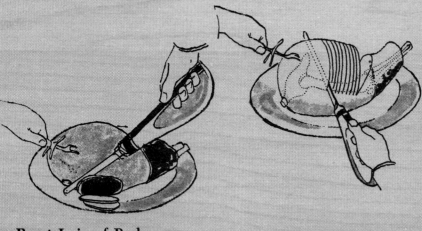

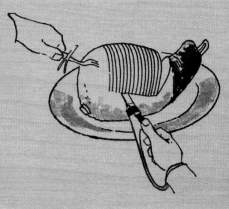

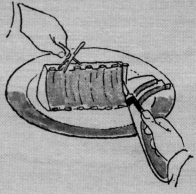

## Roast Loin of Pork

When purchasing roast, ask butcher to separate the backbone from the ribs—this will make carving much easier. *See first diagram.*

The backbone can be easily removed before serving by cutting between rib ends and backbone. *See second diagram.*

Place roast on cutting board or platter with a wooden insert. The rib side should face you. Insert carving fork securely in top of roast. Starting at the right side of roast and cutting close to both sides of each rib, carve thin vertical slices. One slice will have a rib bone and the next will not. *See third diagram.*

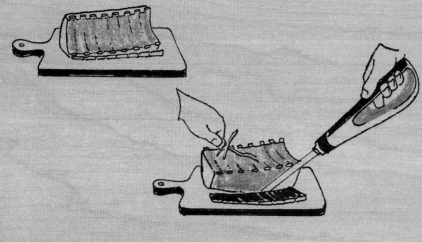

# Roast Leg of Lamb

Place leg of lamb on a heated serving platter. The thick side (or cushion) should be on the left side of the carving surface facing up and the shank bone should be to your right.

Insert carving fork securely in the cushion and carve two or three slices from the thin side which faces you. *See first diagram.*

Rest leg of lamb on the thin cut side where first slices were made. The shank bone is now pointing up. Insert fork securely in left side of roast. Starting at the shank (or right) end, carve ¼- to ½-inch vertical slices straight down almost to the leg bone. *See second diagram.*

(If your electric knife has an adjustable blade, rotate for horizontal carving.) With fork still in meat, start at shank end and run knife along leg bone at right angles to the slices. This will release already carved slices. *See third diagram.* For additional servings, turn platter and slice thin side of roast parallel to the leg bone.

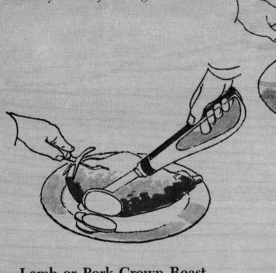

# Lamb or Pork Crown Roast

Place crown on cutting board or platter with a wooden insert. Crown roasts of lamb or pork are carved in the same manner. Set aside any garnish that may interfere with carving. Stuffing should be served with each rib slice.

Insert carving fork securely between two ribs in the left side of crown. Allowing one rib for each slice, carve vertically between two ribs. *See first diagram.*

Lift each slice as it is carved on the knife blade, steadying it with fork, and place on individual serving plate with stuffing. *See second diagram.* Continue carving around crown in the same manner for each serving.

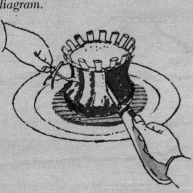

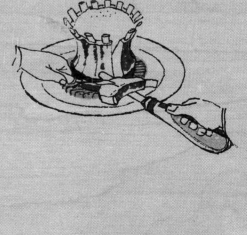

21

### Cushion Lamb Shoulder

There are no bones in this cut and it is often served stuffed. Place meat on cutting board or platter with a wooden insert. The rounded side should face up. Insert carving fork securely in left portion of meat, and carve slices about ½ inch thick including both lamb and stuffing. *See diagram.*

### Picnic Shoulder

Place shoulder on a heated serving platter. The shank end and bone should be to your right. Starting at the shank end, carve as for a baked whole ham (except you need not cut a wedge from the shank end). *See diagram.*

### Beef Tongue

Before serving, skin tongue and remove all excess fat and cartilage from the large end. Place tongue on cutting board or platter with a wooden insert. The rounded side should face you and the tip should be to your left. Insert fork in left portion of tongue. Starting at right, carve thin parallel slices across face of meat at the angle shown. This will allow larger slices from the tip of tongue. *See diagram.*

### Half Ham (Shank End)

Place ham on cutting board or platter with a wooden insert. The shank bone should be to your right and the cushion should face away from you. Remove the cushion section as shown. Rest cushion section on cut surface and carve thin slices, starting at the large end. *See diagram.* For additional servings, remove remaining section by severing the joint. Remove bone and slice as for the cushion section.

### Corned Beef (or Beef Brisket)

Place corned beef on cutting board or platter with a wooden insert. The fat side should be up and the rounded side should face away from you. Remove excess fat. Determine the direction of the grain by looking at the lean side of meat. Insert carving fork securely in left portion of brisket and carve several thin slices at a slight angle across the grain. Rotate brisket as the direction of the fibers changes, always carving across the grain. *See diagram.*

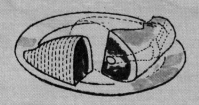

# Roast Turkey or Chicken

Place turkey or chicken on a heated serving platter. The legs should be to your right. Grasp the leg near you and gently pull away while making a vertical cut through the meat and joint between thigh and body. *See first diagram.*

Place leg on another hot platter. Separate thigh from drumstick by cutting at the joint. Slicing parallel to bone, remove the meat from leg. *See second diagram.*

Insert fork into breast of bird. Remove wing by making another vertical cut between the wing and body. *See third diagram.* Place wing on the extra platter.

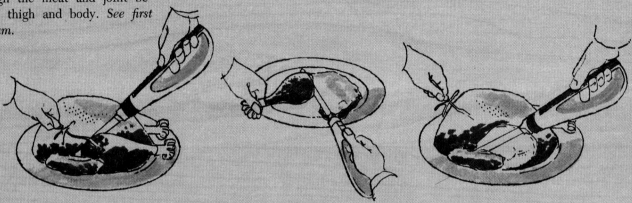

Starting just above the spot where wing was removed, carve thin slices parallel to the breastbone. *See fourth diagram.*

Gradually bring knife blade upward to allow for larger slices as you carve. *See fifth diagram.* For additional servings, turn platter and carve the other side of bird in the same manner.

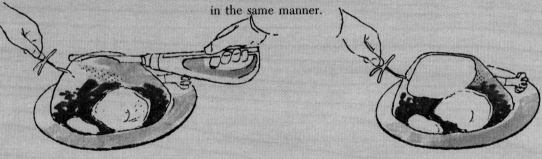

# Roast Goose or Duck

Place goose or duck on a heated serving platter. The legs should be to your right. Remove leg section and wing in the same manner as for a turkey. *See first diagram.*

Insert carving fork to the left of breastbone. Carve long slice parallel to the breastbone. With knife blade slanted towards the ribs, continue making long slices down toward base. *See second diagram.*

(If your electric knife has an adjustable blade, rotate for horizontal carving.) By carving upwards from the base toward the breastbone, all of the parallel slices will be released. *See third diagram.* For additional servings, turn platter and carve the other side of bird in the same manner.

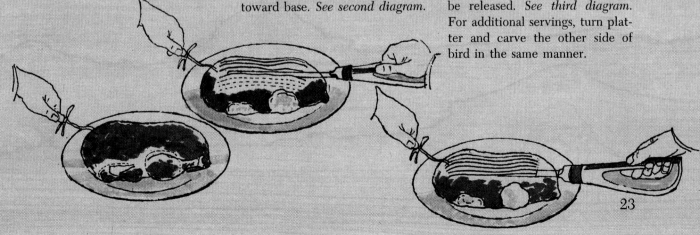

23

Family Favorites for
# EVERY DAY

*Roquefort Stuffed Celery     Olives*
## MEAT LOAF
## ZUCCHINI MOZZARELLA CASSEROLE     *Italian Bread*
## STAR BRIGHT COOKIES
*or Cantaloupe Slices with Lime Wedges*
*Coffee*

## MEAT LOAF

½ cup milk
3 cups bread crumbs
1 pound ground beef
½ pound ground lamb
½ pound ground veal
2 teaspoons salt
⅛ teaspoon pepper
¼ cup finely chopped onion
2 eggs, beaten
1 4-ounce can mushrooms, drained and chopped
1 tablespoon chopped onion
2 tablespoons butter or margarine
½ teaspoon poultry seasoning
¼ teaspoon salt
1 tablespoon chopped parsley

Preheat oven to 350°. Pour milk over 1½ cups of the bread crumbs in mixing bowl. Add ground meats, 2 teaspoons salt, pepper, ¼ cup onion and eggs. Mix thoroughly. Cook mushrooms and 1 tablespoon onion in butter or margarine until lightly browned; add remaining bread crumbs, poultry seasoning, ¼ teaspoon salt and parsley. Mix thoroughly. Place meat mixture on waxed paper and shape into 14x8-inch rectangle. Spread stuffing over meat. Roll lengthwise as for jelly roll and press overlapping edge into roll. Place on rack in shallow roasting pan and bake, uncovered, 1½ hours. Remove from pan and slice into individual servings with electric knife.
*Makes 8 servings.*

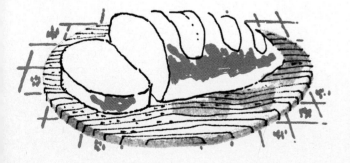

## ZUCCHINI MOZZARELLA CASSEROLE

3-4 medium-sized zucchini, washed
1 large onion, peeled
½ pound mozzarella cheese
2 tablespoons butter or margarine
1 teaspoon onion salt
¼ teaspoon oregano
1 8-ounce can (1 cup) tomato sauce

Preheat oven to 350°. With electric knife, cut zucchini into ½-inch slices and thinly slice onion and mozzarella cheese. Cook zucchini and onion slices together in covered skillet in butter or margarine until tender. Add onion salt, oregano and tomato sauce. Pour into a 1½-quart shallow casserole. Top with mozzarella slices. Bake 30 minutes.

## STAR BRIGHT COOKIES

⅔ cup shortening
1 cup sugar
1 egg, beaten
3½ cups sifted all-purpose flour
3 teaspoons baking powder
½ teaspoon *each* salt and cinnamon
⅓ cup milk
⅓ cup *each* grape and strawberry jelly
⅓ cup peach preserves

Cream shortening in mixing bowl; add sugar and cream until fluffy. Add egg; beat well. Combine flour, baking powder, salt and cinnamon; sift together. Add alternately with milk to creamed mixture. Chill 1 hour.

Preheat oven to 375°. Grease cooky sheets. Roll out dough on lightly floured board to ⅛-inch thickness; with electric knife, cut into 2-inch squares. Place 1 teaspoon jelly or preserves (alternate flavors) in center of half the squares. Make five small slits to form a star in the center of remaining squares; place on top of filled squares and seal edges. Place squares on prepared cooky sheets and bake 12-15 minutes.
*Makes 3-3½ dozen.*

## CORNED BEEF AND CABBAGE

Place 4- to 5-pound corned beef brisket in Dutch oven with 1 bay leaf, 1 clove garlic and 6 peppercorns. Add enough water to cover meat. Bring to a boil over medium heat. Reduce heat; cover and cook over low heat, simmering 4-5 hours until meat is almost fork tender.

With electric knife, cut 1 large head green cabbage into 6 to 8 wedges (removing hard core). About 15 minutes before corned beef is done, add cabbage to meat and cook uncovered 15 minutes longer. Serve meat on hot platter and surround with cabbage wedges. For carving instructions see page 22.

*Makes 6-8 servings.*

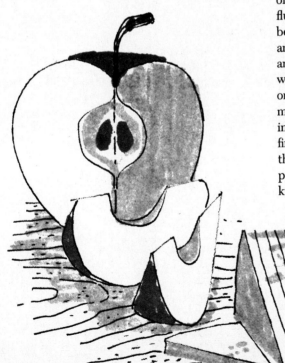

## CREAMY CHEESECAKE

**18 zwieback slices, finely crushed**
**¼ cup butter, melted**
**½ cup sugar**
**2 8-ounce packages cream cheese, softened**
**¼ cup all-purpose flour**
**¼ teaspoon salt**
**4 eggs, separated**
**1 teaspoon grated lemon rind**
**1 tablespoon lemon juice**
**1 cup heavy cream**

Have all ingredients at room temperature. Preheat oven to 325°. Combine zwieback crumbs, butter and 2 tablespoons of the sugar in mixing bowl. Press mixture firmly on bottom and sides of 9-inch springform pan. Chill while making filling.

Beat cheese in large bowl; mix in 2 tablespoons of the sugar, flour and salt; beat until light and fluffy. Beat egg yolks until thick and lemon-colored; beat into cheese mixture. Stir in lemon rind, juice and cream. (Or put ingredients in blender container and run on speed 6 or high until smooth.) Beat egg whites until soft peaks form; beat in remaining sugar, one tablespoon at a time, and continue beating until mixture holds its shape. Fold into cheese mixture. Pour into prepared pan. Bake 1½ hours or until center is firm. Turn off heat; let stand in oven 1 hour. Cool thoroughly before removing from pan. Remove from pan and cut into individual servings with electric knife.

BARBECUED RIB STEAKS<br/>
Baked Potatoes with Sour Cream<br/>
Lemon-buttered Lima Beans   TOMATOES VINAIGRETTE<br/>
Garlic Bread or Hard Rolls<br/>
CINNAMON CAKE or Pear Halves with Chocolate Sauce<br/>
Coffee

## BARBECUED RIB STEAKS

1 clove garlic
½ cup vegetable oil
2 3-pound rib steaks, bone removed
1 teaspoon dry mustard
½ teaspoon freshly ground black pepper
1¾ teaspoons salt
2 teaspoons Worcestershire sauce
¼ cup all-purpose flour
1 cup light brown sugar
1 tablespoon butter or margarine

Crush garlic clove into oil; set aside for 1 hour. Brush both sides of steaks with garlic oil. Let stand 1 hour at room temperature. Combine mustard, pepper, salt, Worcestershire sauce and flour in a mixing bowl. Place steaks on a board. Score and gash fat around the edges every 2 inches to prevent curling. Divide spicy mixture into four parts. Spread fourth of mixture on side of each steak. Using back of cleaver or wooden mallet, pound mixture into meat. Repeat procedure on second sides of steaks. Let stand 30 minutes. Knead the light brown sugar into each side of steak. Place steaks on broiling rack 3 inches from heat and broil until both sides are dark brown, turning frequently. Remove from broiler; lift off glazed sugar coating. Serve steaks dotted with butter on hot platter. Slice with electric knife. During carving, juice from meat will blend with butter, making a light gravy to serve over meat.
*Makes 6-8 servings.*

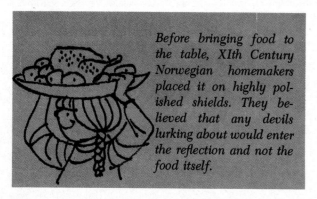

*Before bringing food to the table, XIth Century Norwegian homemakers placed it on highly polished shields. They believed that any devils lurking about would enter the reflection and not the food itself.*

## TOMATOES VINAIGRETTE

½ cup French dressing (oil and vinegar type)
1 tablespoon dried parsley flakes
1 tablespoon chopped green pepper
2 tablespoons chopped pickle
1 teaspoon chopped chives
½ teaspoon paprika
Sliced tomatoes

Combine all ingredients except tomatoes in covered jar and shake well before using. Serve over sliced tomatoes.
*Makes ⅔ cup.*

## CINNAMON CAKE

½ cup butter or margarine
1 cup sugar
2 eggs
1 teaspoon vanilla
2 cups sifted all-purpose flour
1 teaspoon baking powder
1 teaspoon baking soda
1 teaspoon salt
1 cup dairy sour cream
Topping (below)

Preheat oven to 350°. Grease 9-inch springform pan. Cream butter or margarine in mixing bowl. Add sugar, eggs and vanilla; cream until light and fluffy. Sift flour, baking powder, soda and salt together, and add to creamed mixture alternately with sour cream. Pour half of batter into prepared pan; sprinkle with half of Topping. Spread with remaining batter and sprinkle with remaining Topping. Bake 45-50 minutes. Cool in pan. Remove from pan and cool thoroughly on rack. Place cake on board and cut into individual servings with electric knife.

**Topping:**

Combine ¾ cup chopped nuts, ⅓ cup sugar and 1½ teaspoons cinnamon in mixing bowl.

*Pickle Relish Tray*
## RICE BAKED STUFFED FISH
*Lemon Wedges     Peas and Pearl Onions     Corn Muffins*
*Cucumber and Tomato Salad     SPICY DRESSING*
*PECAN APPLE TORTE or Fruit Compote*
*Coffee*

## RICE BAKED STUFFED FISH

1 3- to 4-pound pike, perch or whitefish, cleaned
    and boned
¼ cup butter or margarine
2 tablespoons minced onion
¼ cup dry bread crumbs
1½ cups cooked rice
Salt and pepper
Paprika
½ teaspoon basil
¼ teaspoon dill weed or seed
1 tablespoon minced parsley
1 tablespoon lemon juice
¼ cup melted butter or margarine
2 slices lemon, cut in half

Preheat oven to 350°. Grease shallow baking pan. Melt ¼ cup butter or margarine in skillet. Cook onion until tender. Remove from heat. Add crumbs, rice, ½ teaspoon salt, ⅛ teaspoon pepper, ¼ teaspoon paprika, basil, dill weed, parsley and lemon juice. Toss lightly until mixed.

Fill cavity lightly with stuffing and fasten with skewers and string. Spread half of melted butter or margarine over entire fish. Sprinkle with 1 teaspoon salt and ¼ teaspoon pepper.

Place half slices of lemon in center of prepared pan. Place fish on lemon slices; sprinkle with ⅛ teaspoon paprika. Bake 45 minutes or until fish flakes easily when tested with a fork. Baste frequently with melted butter during last 15 minutes. Serve on heated platter; garnish with additional lemon slices and parsley. Cut into individual servings with electric knife.
*Makes 6 servings.*

## SPICY DRESSING

6 tablespoons wine vinegar
1 cup vegetable oil
1 teaspoon salt
½ teaspoon ground cumin
1 clove garlic

Put all ingredients in blender container; cover and run on speed 5 (or high) about 30 seconds. (Or crush garlic clove and put all ingredients in covered jar; shake well.)
*Makes 1¼ cups.*

## PECAN APPLE TORTE

2 pounds apples, pared, cored and sliced (6 cups)
2 tablespoons water
2 tablespoons lemon juice
1 cup sugar
½ cup butter, softened
4 eggs, separated
¾ teaspoon vanilla
1¼ cups finely chopped pecans
1 cup heavy cream, chilled and whipped
Maraschino cherries

Preheat oven to 350°. Line 8x8x2-inch pan with foil. Combine apples, water, lemon juice and ½ cup of the sugar in 2-quart saucepan. Cover and cook over low heat just until tender; drain and arrange slices in bottom of prepared pan. Mix remaining sugar, butter and egg yolks in mixing bowl; stir in vanilla and pecans. Fold in stiffly beaten egg whites. Spread batter over apples and bake 45 minutes or until top is firm when lightly touched. Chill. Turn out on board. With electric knife, cut into squares and top with whipped cream; garnish with maraschino cherries.

Basil

Dill

Parsley

Cumin

*Barley Soup     Sesame Seed Crackers*
SAUERBRATEN     *Gingersnap Gravy*
*Red Cabbage*     POTATO PANCAKES     *Applesauce*
ORANGE TORTE *or Vanilla Ice Cream and Fig Cookies*
*Cold Beer     Coffee*

### SAUERBRATEN

3 tablespoons flour
1 tablespoon salt
¼ teaspoon pepper
1 3- to 4-pound arm or blade pot roast
3 tablespoons shortening
¼ cup vinegar
¼ cup water
1 large onion, sliced ¼ inch thick
1 bay leaf
¼ teaspoon *each* allspice, cinnamon and ground cloves
½ cup raisins
¼ cup gingersnap crumbs

Mix together flour, salt and pepper. Dredge roast with seasoned flour. Melt shortening in a Dutch oven and brown meat on both sides. Pour off drippings. Add vinegar, water, onion, bay leaf and spices. Cover tightly and simmer 3 hours. Remove bay leaf. Add raisins and continue cooking 30 minutes or longer until meat is tender and raisins are soft. Thicken liquid from meat with gingersnap crumbs. Let sauerbraten stand 10 minutes before slicing. Serve with Gingersnap Gravy. See carving instructions for blade pot roast on page 19.
*Makes 6-8 servings.*

### POTATO PANCAKES

3 cups grated potatoes (about 6 medium)
2 eggs, beaten
¼ cup sifted all-purpose flour
1 tablespoon grated onion
Salt and pepper
⅛ teaspoon baking powder
½ cup milk
3 tablespoons butter or margarine

Combine all ingredients except butter. Mix thoroughly Pour small amounts onto a hot, buttered griddle or skillet. Fry until brown, turning once.
*Makes 18 pancakes.*

### ORANGE TORTE

1 cup butter or margarine
1½ cups sugar
3 eggs
2½ cups sifted all-purpose flour
1 teaspoon baking soda
½ teaspoon baking powder
½ teaspoon salt
1½ cups nuts, chopped
1 cup buttermilk
2 tablespoons grated orange rind
1 cup orange juice

Have all ingredients room temperature. Preheat oven to 375°. Grease 9-inch tube pan. Cream butter or margarine in mixing bowl. Add 1 cup of the sugar gradually, beating until light and fluffy. Add eggs, one at a time, beating thoroughly after each addition. Sift together flour, soda, baking powder and salt; dredge nuts in ¼ cup of mixture. Combine buttermilk, orange rind and ½ cup of the juice. Add remaining dry ingredients to creamed mixture alternately with buttermilk mixture. Fold nuts into mixture. Pour into prepared pan and bake 1 hour.

Let torte stand in pan 30 minutes after removing from oven. Remove cake from pan to rack; place rack over platter. Pour combined remaining orange juice and sugar slowly over cake, and continue to baste with syrup which drains off cake onto platter. Transfer torte to serving plate and cut into wedges with electric knife.

*Chilled Clam Juice*
# BAKED COD WITH SOUR CREAM STUFFING
*Olives and Watermelon Pickles*     *Lemon Slices*
*Mashed Potatoes*    SPINACH WITH BRAZIL NUT TOPPING
DATE LOAF *or Caramel Pudding*
*Coffee*

## BAKED COD WITH SOUR CREAM STUFFING

1 4-pound cod, cleaned and boned
½ teaspoon salt
1 2-ounce can sliced mushrooms, drained
⅓ cup diced onion
¼ cup butter or margarine
2 cups dry bread cubes
1 cup dairy sour cream
1 tablespoon chopped dill pickle
1 teaspoon paprika
½ teaspoon salt
⅛ teaspoon pepper
3 tablespoons butter or margarine, melted
Lemon slices
Dill pickle slices
Parsley

Preheat oven to 350°. Line shallow baking pan with foil and grease. Rub inside of fish with salt. Sauté mushrooms and onion in butter. Combine with bread cubes in mixing bowl. Add sour cream, pickle, paprika, salt and pepper. Fill cod with stuffing and fasten with skewers and string. Place fish in prepared pan. Brush with melted butter and bake approximately 50-60 minutes, basting with butter every 15 minutes. Arrange cod on warm serving platter; garnish with lemon slices, dill pickle slices and parsley. Cut into individual servings with electric knife.
*Makes 6 servings.*

## SPINACH WITH BRAZIL NUT TOPPING

⅓ cup butter or margarine
⅓ cup soft bread crumbs
¼ cup chopped Brazil nuts
Dash freshly ground black pepper
2 10-ounce packages frozen spinach, cooked

Melt butter or margarine in a small saucepan. Add bread crumbs and Brazil nuts. Stir and cook until crumbs are brown. Add pepper. Serve over hot cooked spinach.
*Makes 6 servings.*

## DATE LOAF

2 cups sifted all-purpose flour
1 teaspoon baking powder
¼ teaspoon salt
¾ cup butter or margarine
1 cup firmly packed brown sugar
2 eggs, beaten
½ teaspoon baking soda
½ cup milk
1 teaspoon vanilla
1 pound pitted dates, chopped
½ cup chopped pecans
1 cup heavy cream, whipped

Preheat oven to 350°. Line the bottom of a 9x5x3-inch loaf pan with waxed paper. Sift flour, baking powder and salt together. In mixing bowl, cream butter or margarine with brown sugar until light and fluffy. Add beaten eggs. Dissolve soda in milk and add with vanilla to creamed mixture. Add chopped dates and nuts to flour mixture. Stir into creamed mixture. Mix well. Turn batter into prepared pan; bake 50-60 minutes or until done. Cool in pan 5 minutes. Remove from pan and cool thoroughly on rack. When cake is cool, turn out onto serving plate. Slice with electric knife and serve with whipped cream.

*PICNIC SHOULDER WITH CORN BREAD STUFFING*

*Hot Applesauce     Italian Green Beans     Pickles*

*SUNSHINE TREATS*

*or Butter Pecan Ice Cream and Lemon Cookies*

*Coffee or Tea*

## PICNIC SHOULDER WITH CORN BREAD STUFFING

¼ cup chopped onion
¼ cup butter or margarine
½ cup chopped celery
1 tablespoon chopped fresh parsley
½ teaspoon salt
½ teaspoon sage
1½ cups croutons
1 cup day-old corn bread crumbs
¼ cup hot water
1 3- to 5-pound cushion-style picnic shoulder,
   boned and sewed on two sides
Salt and pepper

Preheat oven to 300-325°. Sauté onion in butter or margarine until tender and transparent. Add celery, parsley, salt, sage, croutons and corn bread crumbs. Mix well. Stir in hot water.

Season pork shoulder inside and out with salt and pepper. Fill pocket of meat with stuffing and close with skewers and thread. Place shoulder, fat side up, on rack in uncovered roasting pan. Roast until meat thermometer registers 160° (40-45 minutes per pound) or until done. Serve on heated platter. See carving instructions on page 22.

*Makes 6-8 servings.*

## SUNSHINE TREATS

1¼ cups chopped dates
½ cup water
½ cup sugar
1 tablespoon lemon juice
¼ cup chopped walnuts
½ cup butter or margarine
1 cup firmly packed brown sugar
1 egg, beaten
1 teaspoon lemon juice
½ teaspoon vanilla
2¼ cups sifted all-purpose flour
½ teaspoon baking soda
½ teaspoon salt

Combine dates, water, ½ cup sugar, 1 tablespoon lemon juice and walnuts in small bowl. Set aside.

Cream butter or margarine in mixing bowl; add brown sugar gradually and combine until light and fluffy. Add egg and mix well. Stir in 1 teaspoon lemon juice and vanilla. Combine flour, baking soda and salt; sift into creamed mixture. Blend well. Chill dough thoroughly. Divide in half and roll each portion into rectangle ¼ inch thick on floured pastry cloth. Spread with date mixture. Roll up as for jelly roll and refrigerate until firm.

Preheat oven to 400°. Grease cooky sheets. Place each roll on board and cut into thin slices with electric knife. Bake on prepared cooky sheets 8-10 minutes.

*Makes about 4 dozen.*

The envelopes used by English nobility in the XVth Century were made of bread dough. After the messenger delivered the letter he was allowed to keep the dough envelope as a tip.

*SHERRIED CREAM OF MUSHROOM SOUP*
*ROAST TURKEY ROLL*
*Gravy     Wild Rice     Spiced Fruits*
*Tomato and Cauliflower Salad     TANGY DRESSING*
*PECAN FILLED ANGEL CAKE*
*Coffee*

## SHERRIED CREAM OF MUSHROOM SOUP

¼ pound fresh mushrooms, washed and sliced
⅓ cup finely chopped onion
1 clove garlic, minced
¼ cup butter or margarine
1 tablespoon lemon juice
3 tablespoons flour
1¾ cups chicken bouillon
¼ cup sherry
2 teaspoons salt
¼ teaspoon pepper
2 cups light cream

Sauté mushrooms, onion and garlic in butter or margarine in saucepan. Stir in lemon juice and flour. Gradually stir in bouillon, sherry and seasonings. Cook over low heat until slightly thickened, stirring constantly. Stir in cream; continue cooking until hot, being careful not to let soup boil.

*Makes 6 servings.*

## ROAST TURKEY ROLL

1 3- to 9-pound boneless turkey roll
1 teaspoon salt
¼ teaspoon pepper
½ cup butter or margarine, melted

Preheat oven to 350°. Rub turkey roll with salt and pepper. Place on rack in shallow baking pan; brush entire roll with melted butter or margarine and cook, uncovered, basting occasionally with additional melted butter or pan drippings. Follow chart below for approximate cooking time, or roast until meat thermometer registers 170°-175°. Lengthen cooking time approximately ½ hour for cooking frozen roll. If desired, pan drippings may be used to make gravy. Slice with electric knife and serve.

| | |
|---|---|
| 3-5 pounds | 2-2½ hours |
| 5-7 pounds | 2½-3½ hours |
| 7-9 pounds | 3¼-4 hours |

## TANGY DRESSING

¾ cup vegetable oil
½ teaspoon salt
¼ teaspoon *each* garlic salt, onion salt and celery salt
½ teaspoon dry mustard
⅛ teaspoon pepper
½ teaspoon dill seed
½ thin slice onion
¼ cup cider vinegar
1 tablespoon fresh lemon juice

Put all ingredients in blender container; cover and run on speed 5 (or high) until mixed. (Or finely chop onion. Combine all ingredients and mix well.) Store in covered jar in the refrigerator.

*Makes 1 cup.*

## PECAN FILLED ANGEL CAKE

1 10-inch angel food cake
1 quart butter pecan ice cream, softened
1 cup heavy cream
¼ cup sugar
⅓ cup chopped toasted pecans

Place cake on board or heavy foil. With electric knife, slice a layer of cake about 1 inch from top; set aside. Make a hollow in cake by cutting down into it 1 inch from the outer edge and 1 inch from the middle hole, leaving a substantial 1-inch base on bottom of cake. Remove excess cake to form a cavity. Spoon ice cream into cavity in cake; replace top of cake and press down against ice cream. Wrap cake in foil and freeze until firm but not hard (about 2 hours).

Whip cream until soft peaks form. Add sugar, whipping until stiff. Frost top and sides of cake with sweetened whipped cream. Garnish with pecans. Freeze for at least ½ hour longer. Cut into wedges with electric knife.

*CREAM OF BROCCOLI SOUP*    *Cheese Wafers*
*FRUITED POT ROAST*
*Butterflake Rolls*
*Green Salad*    *SUPERB DRESSING*
*COFFEE ICE CREAM CAKE ROLL*
*Coffee or Tea*

## CREAM OF BROCCOLI SOUP

1 small onion, thinly sliced
1 leek, thinly sliced (white part only)
1 small stalk celery, sliced (without leaves)
1 tablespoon butter
½ cup water
2 10-ounce packages frozen chopped broccoli
2 teaspoons salt
Dash cayenne
2 tablespoons uncooked rice
2 cups chicken broth
½ cup cream or milk

Put onion, leek, celery, butter and water in 2-quart saucepan; simmer slowly 2 minutes over medium heat. In separate saucepan cook broccoli until tender and drain (reserve ½ cup liquid).

Add salt, cayenne, rice and 1 cup chicken broth to onion mixture in saucepan; simmer 15 minutes. Do not boil. Pour chicken broth-onion mixture into blender container; cover and run on speed 7 (or high) until liquefied. Pour back into saucepan.

Put broccoli and remaining chicken broth in blender container; cover and run on speed 7 (or high) until broccoli is liquefied. If mixture becomes too thick to flow, add the reserved broccoli cooking liquid to thin. Add broccoli to onion mixture in saucepan; add cream. Heat (do not boil) and serve.
*Makes 8-10 servings.*

## FRUITED POT ROAST

1 4-pound pot roast
2 teaspoons salt
¼ teaspoon pepper
2 tablespoons sugar
1 cup apple cider
2 medium onions, sliced
2 tablespoons mixed pickling spices
12 dried prunes
12 dried apricots

Brown beef on all sides in 4-quart Dutch oven over high heat. Season with salt, pepper and sugar. Add cider and onion slices. Tie pickling spices in a cheese-cloth bag and place in liquid in Dutch oven. Cover and simmer meat 3-3½ hours over low heat or until tender.

Cover prunes and apricots with water; soak while meat is cooking. When meat is tender, drain water from fruit. Place fruit on roast and continue cooking 30 minutes longer. Drain liquid from meat and fruit. Discard bag of spices. For gravy to serve with roast, thicken liquid with equal parts of flour and butter creamed together; serve gravy separately. Serve meat and fruit on heated platter. For carving instructions see page 19.
*Makes 6-8 servings.*

## SUPERB DRESSING

3 egg yolks
1 tablespoon dry mustard
¾ teaspoon salt
1 tablespoon vinegar
¾ cup vegetable oil

Put all ingredients in blender container; cover and run on speed 4 (or low) about 30 seconds. (Or place all ingredients in covered jar and shake well.)
*Makes 1 cup.*

## COFFEE ICE CREAM CAKE ROLL

Confectioners' sugar
4 eggs, separated
¾ cup sugar
1 teaspoon vanilla
¾ cup sifted cake flour
¾ teaspoon baking powder
¼ teaspoon salt
1 quart coffee ice cream
Meringue (right)

Preheat oven to 375°. Grease a 15½x10½x1-inch jelly roll pan. Line pan with greased waxed paper. Sprinkle a long clean tea towel or cloth evenly with confectioners' sugar.

Beat egg yolks until light and lemon-colored in mixing bowl. Beat in sugar until well mixed; add vanilla. Sift flour and baking powder together; add slowly to egg yolk mixture, beating until smooth. Add salt to egg whites; beat until stiff but not dry. Fold lightly into batter. Spread dough in prepared pan. Bake 13 minutes. Invert cake on prepared tea towel. Remove waxed paper from bottom of cake. If edges are brown and crisp, trim off. Roll cake up in towel. Let stand until cool. Carefully unroll towel and spread cake with softened ice cream. Reroll and freeze until firm. Just before serving, preheat oven to 450°. Remove ice cream roll from freezer. Frost roll completely with Meringue. Place on board and bake in oven 3 minutes or until meringue is lightly browned. Slice with electric knife and serve immediately.

**Meringue:**

Have 4 egg whites at room temperature. Add ¼ teaspoon salt and beat until frothy. Add ½ cup sugar, two tablespoons at a time, and beat until mixture becomes shiny and stiff.

37

*Cold Vichyssoise*

## ALSATIAN ROAST CHICKEN

*Peas with Mushrooms     Buttered French Rolls*

*Endive Salad*

*APPLE KUCHEN or Cheese and Fresh Fruit*

*Coffee*

### ALSATIAN ROAST CHICKEN

1 5-pound roasting chicken with liver
2 tablespoons vegetable oil
2 slices bread
1 cup milk
3 tablespoons butter
2 tablespoons parsley, finely chopped
2 tablespoons chives, finely chopped
4 egg yolks
Salt and pepper
Dash thyme
2 tablespoons butter, melted
2 cups bread crumbs

Preheat oven to 300°. Wash chicken and pat dry with absorbent paper. Rub cavity with salt and set aside.

Sauté liver in oil in small skillet until browned; drain and mince. Set aside.

Soak bread slices in milk, then squeeze and separate with fork. Combine liver, butter, parsley, chives, 2 of the egg yolks, bread, salt, pepper and thyme in a mixing bowl; mix thoroughly. Stuff cavity lightly with mixture; skewer the openings closed, and truss and tie the legs. Place fowl on a rack in an uncovered shallow roasting pan. Bake 2½-3 hours (30-35 minutes per pound) or until tender and golden brown.

While fowl is roasting, combine remaining egg yolks with melted butter. Add salt and pepper to taste. When fowl is almost done, remove from oven and brush with this mixture. Sprinkle and pat fowl with bread crumbs and return to oven. Roast 10 minutes longer or until crumbs are golden brown. Remove skewers and string; serve chicken on heated platter. To carve, see instructions for turkey on page 23.

*Makes 6-8 servings.*

### APPLE KUCHEN

1 cup all-purpose flour
½ teaspoon baking powder
¼ teaspoon salt
2 tablespoons sugar
2½ tablespoons butter or margarine, softened
2 eggs, beaten
2 tablespoons milk
5 cups sliced apples (4 large)
½ cup seedless raisins
⅔ cup sugar
1 teaspoon cinnamon
1 tablespoon grated orange rind
Whipped cream

Preheat oven to 425°. Grease 8-inch springform pan. Sift flour, baking powder, salt and 2 tablespoons sugar together in mixing bowl. Cut in butter until mixture is crumbly. Add eggs and mix well. Slowly add milk, stirring constantly. Spread dough on bottom and partly up sides of prepared pan with spatula.

Place apples and raisins in saucepan with water to cover. Cook until apples are tender but not mushy; drain. Combine ⅔ cup sugar, cinnamon and lemon rind. Add to apples and raisins. Stir thoroughly. Spoon fruit mixture on top of pastry in prepared pan. Bake 50-60 minutes or until filling is firm and crust is golden brown. Remove cake from pan to board and cut into individual servings with electric knife. Serve topped with whipped cream.

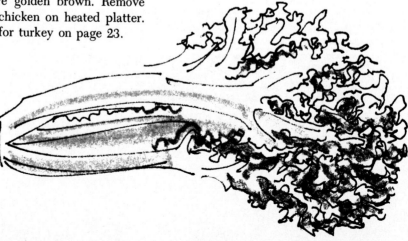

*Raw Vegetable Relishes*
## VEAL RUMP ROAST WITH CREOLE SAUCE
## POTATOES AU GRATIN
*Salt Sticks*   WALDORF SALAD SUPREME
## CHOCOLATE NUT TRIANGLES
*Coffee*

## VEAL RUMP ROAST
## WITH CREOLE SAUCE

1 3- to 4-pound veal rump roast
Salt and pepper
4 slices bacon
Creole Sauce (below)

Preheat oven to 300°. Place roast on rack in open roasting pan. Season with salt and pepper. Place bacon slices on roast. Do not add water. Roast, uncovered, 2½-3½ hours or until meat thermometer registers 170° (45-50 minutes per pound). Slice with electric knife and serve with Creole Sauce.
*Makes 6-8 servings.*

Creole Sauce:

¼ cup finely chopped onion
½ cup green pepper strips
1 small clove garlic, minced
3 tablespoons drippings from roast
1 tablespoon flour
1 16-ounce can (2 cups) tomatoes, cut in small
  pieces
1 4-ounce can (½ cup) sliced mushrooms (reserve
  liquid)
⅛ teaspoon pepper
½ teaspoon salt
1 teaspoon sugar
1 tablespoon chopped parsley

Cook onion, green pepper and garlic in pan drippings in skillet about 5 minutes or until tender. Stir in flour. Add tomatoes, mushrooms, reserved liquid, pepper, salt and sugar. Cook until thickened. Add parsley.

## POTATOES AU GRATIN

¼ cup butter or margarine, melted
¼ cup sifted all-purpose flour
1 teaspoon salt
⅛ teaspoon pepper
2 cups milk
1 cup freshly grated sharp cheese
2 pounds (4 cups) cooked diced potatoes, seasoned
  with salt and pepper
2 tablespoons butter or margarine, melted
¼ cup dry bread crumbs
1 tablespoon parsley

Preheat oven to 375°. Grease a 1½-quart casserole. Combine ¼ cup melted butter or margarine, flour and seasonings in saucepan; cook over low heat, stirring until smooth. Add milk gradually, stirring constantly; add cheese. Cook about 5 minutes or until sauce thickens, stirring occasionally. Combine sauce and potatoes; place in prepared casserole. Mix 2 tablespoons melted butter or margarine, bread crumbs and parsley. Sprinkle on top of potatoes. Bake 20 minutes or until browned and thoroughly hot.
*Makes 6-8 servings.*

## WALDORF SALAD SUPREME

4 cups unpeeled red apples, cored and cubed
2 cups sliced celery
1 cup broken walnuts
1 cup dairy sour cream
½ cup mayonnaise
¼ pound Roquefort cheese, coarsely crumbled
Salad greens

Combine apples, celery and walnuts in mixing bowl. Stir sour cream and mayonnaise into mixture; add crumbled cheese. Toss until well mixed. Serve on crisp salad greens.
*Makes 8 servings.*

## CHOCOLATE NUT TRIANGLES

⅔ cup shortening
2¼ cups firmly packed brown sugar (1 pound)
3 eggs
2⅔ cups sifted all-purpose flour
2½ teaspoons baking powder
½ teaspoon salt
1 cup chopped nuts
1 6-ounce package (1 cup) semisweet chocolate
  pieces
Maple Frosting (below)
Chocolate Frosting (below)
Candied cherries and nuts

Preheat oven to 350°. Line 15½x10½x1-inch jelly roll
pan with foil. Melt shortening in large saucepan. Stir
in brown sugar; mix well. Remove from heat; cool
10 minutes. Beat in eggs, one at a time. Sift flour,
baking powder and salt together; stir into sugar mixture. Stir in nuts and chocolate pieces. Spread in prepared pan. Bake 25-30 minutes. Cool 10 minutes in
pan; invert on board. Cool thoroughly. Frost half
with Maple Frosting and half with Chocolate Frosting. With electric knife, trim edges and cut into 2-inch
squares. Cut each square diagonally to form triangles.
Decorate with nuts and candied cherries.
*Makes approximately 6 dozen.*

Maple Frosting:

½ cup confectioners' sugar
Dash cream of tartar
1 tablespoon egg white
¼ teaspoon maple flavoring

Sift together confectioners' sugar and cream of tartar;
add egg white and flavoring. Beat until frosting holds
its shape. Cover with damp cloth when not in use.

Chocolate Frosting:

¼ cup evaporated milk
Dash salt
½ cup (3 ounces) semisweet chocolate pieces
½ teaspoon vanilla

Combine evaporated milk and salt in saucepan. Bring
just to a boil. Remove from heat. Add chocolate pieces;
stir until melted. Add vanilla. Cool.

## Relish Ideas

Mix and match any of the following for a taste-
tempting, colorful relish platter. Or serve them
as an appetizer or hors d'oeuvre with salted
sour cream or your favorite dip.

*Carrot and celery strips*
*Cauliflowerets*
*Radish roses*
*Cherry tomatoes*
*Green pepper strips or rings*
*Scallions or green onions*
*Cucumber slices or wedges*
*Ripe olives*
*Pimiento-stuffed green olives*
*Cheese cubes or wedges*
*Pineapple sticks*
*Apple and pear wedges*
*Melon cubes*
*Sweet and sour pickle chips*
*Dill pickle fans*
*Watermelon pickles*
*Pickled mushrooms or beet slices*
*Marinated onion or cucumber slices*

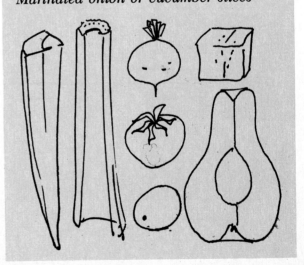

41

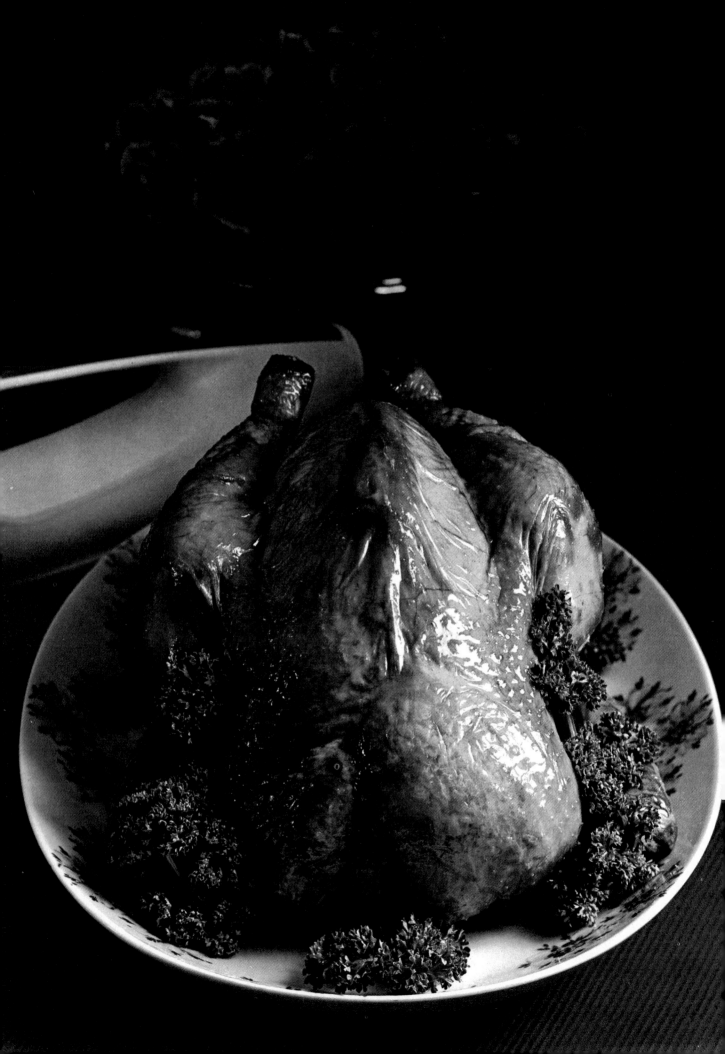

*Carrot and Celery Sticks, Sweet Pickle Chips*
### ROAST CAPON
*Mashed Potatoes     Gravy*

*Green Beans Parmesan*

## BUTTERSCOTCH COOKIES    *Fruit Gelatin*

*Coffee*

## ROAST CAPON

1 6-pound capon
1 tablespoon salt
1 pound fresh mushrooms, washed and sliced
3 tablespoons butter
1 pound almonds, finely ground
2 cups soft bread crumbs
3 eggs, lightly beaten
2 tablespoons butter, melted
1 teaspoon salt
Dash pepper
1 cup thick white sauce
2 tablespoons sherry
Dash nutmeg
1 teaspoon sugar

Preheat oven to 325°. Rub cavity of fowl with 1 tablespoon salt.

In skillet, sauté mushrooms in 3 tablespoons butter until done. Combine mushrooms, almonds, bread crumbs, eggs, melted butter, salt and pepper in mixing bowl. Blend white sauce, sherry, nutmeg and sugar. Add to mushroom mixture. Mix well. Stuff cavity and fasten with skewers and string; truss. Place capon on rack in roasting pan and roast, uncovered, 3-3½ hours (30 minutes per pound). Remove skewers and string; serve capon on heated platter. To carve see instructions for turkey on page 23.

*Makes 6-8 servings.*

## BUTTERSCOTCH COOKIES

½ cup butter or margarine
1 cup firmly packed brown sugar
1 egg, beaten
½ teaspoon vanilla
2 cups sifted all-purpose flour
½ teaspoon cream of tartar
½ teaspoon baking powder
½ cup chopped nuts

Combine butter or margarine, brown sugar, egg and vanilla in mixing bowl; cream until fluffy. Sift together flour, cream of tartar and baking powder. Add to creamed mixture. Stir in nuts. Shape into 2-inch rolls; wrap in waxed paper. Chill 2-3 hours.

Preheat oven to 400°. Place dough on board and cut into ⅛-inch slices with electric knife; place on ungreased cooky sheet. Bake 8-10 minutes.

*Makes 4 dozen.*

## BAKED HAM SHANK WITH APPLESAUCE GLAZE

Scalloped Potatoes    FRENCH FRIED GREEN PEPPERS

Shredded Lettuce with Russian Dressing

### BANANA STRAWBERRY TORTE

or Sliced Bananas, Vanilla Ice Cream and Strawberry Sauce

Coffee

### BAKED HAM SHANK WITH APPLESAUCE GLAZE

Preheat oven to 325°. Place a 5- to 6-pound ham shank, fat side up, on rack in open roasting pan. Do not add water. Roast, uncovered, 3-3½ hours. Remove from oven and spread Applesauce Glaze (below) over meat. Return to oven 20-30 minutes or until meat thermometer registers 160°. Serve glazed ham on heated platter. For carving instructions see page 22. *Makes 6-8 servings.*

**Applesauce Glaze:**

1 cup applesauce
2 tablespoons honey
¼ teaspoon ginger
1 teaspoon cinnamon
2 tablespoons lemon juice

Combine all ingredients except lemon juice in saucepan. Cook slowly, stirring occasionally, until thoroughly hot. Stir in lemon juice.

### FRENCH FRIED GREEN PEPPERS

1 pound (4 large) green peppers, washed and seeded
¾ cup bread crumbs
1 tablespoon salt
½ teaspoon ground oregano
¼ teaspoon pepper
⅔ cup grated Parmesan cheese
2 eggs
¼ cup water

With electric knife, cut green peppers into rings ½ inch thick; then cut each ring in half or into thirds, depending on size. Combine crumbs, salt, oregano, pepper and cheese in small mixing bowl. Beat eggs and water together in another small bowl. Dip green pepper slices into crumbs, then into egg mixture and again into crumbs. Chill 1 hour. Fry in skillet in ½ inch hot oil (375°) until tender and lightly browned on all sides. Drain on absorbent paper. *Makes 6-8 servings.*

### BANANA STRAWBERRY TORTE

1 10-inch angel food cake
½ cup dairy sour cream
¼ cup sugar
¼ cup crushed strawberries
½ cup sliced strawberries
1¼ cups sliced bananas
1 cup heavy cream, whipped
Strawberry halves

Slice cake crosswise into three equal layers. Combine sour cream, sugar and crushed strawberries. Fold sliced strawberries, ¾ cup of the bananas and sour cream mixture into whipped cream; chill 30 minutes or until mixture starts to thicken. Spread about ½ cup fruit mixture on each layer, including top of cake; stack layers. Chill.

To serve, garnish top of cake with remaining banana slices and strawberry halves. Cut into wedges with electric knife.

Fun and Fancy
BUFFET
DINNERS

## BEEF A LA RUSSE

2 pounds round steak
⅔ cup finely chopped onion
1 clove garlic, crushed
3 tablespoons bacon fat
1 4-ounce can sliced mushrooms, undrained
1 cup dairy sour cream
1 8-ounce can tomato sauce
1 cup beef bouillon
1 teaspoon salt
⅛ teaspoon pepper
1 tablespoon Worcestershire sauce
2 tablespoons all-purpose flour
2 tablespoons water

With electric knife cut steak into 1-inch cubes.° Sauté onion and garlic in bacon fat in 10-inch skillet over low heat until onion is tender. Add steak cubes and cook until browned. Add mushrooms with liquid, sour cream, tomato sauce, bouillon, salt, pepper and Worcestershire sauce. Cover and cook slowly over low heat 2 hours.

Blend flour and water together and stir into meat mixture; cook about 1 minute until mixture thickens. Serve garnished with parsley, if desired.
*Makes 8 servings.*

°Meat is easier to cut if partially frozen.

## MINTED CARROTS

5-6 carrots, sliced (3 cups)
¼ cup melted butter or margarine
1 teaspoon sugar
½ teaspoon salt
1 tablespoon minced mint leaves
Sprig of mint

Place carrots and 1 cup water in a 1½-quart saucepan; cover and cook over medium heat. When water begins to boil, reduce heat to low; continue cooking 20-30 minutes or until carrots are tender; drain.

Combine butter, sugar, salt and minced mint leaves in a bowl. Pour over drained carrots. Garnish with sprig of mint.
*Makes 4 servings.*

## APPLE CHERRY NUT BREAD

⅔ cup butter or margarine
1⅓ cups sugar
4 eggs
2 cups canned applesauce
½ cup milk
4 cups sifted all-purpose flour
2 teaspoons baking powder
1 teaspoon *each* baking soda and salt
2 tablespoons grated lemon rind
1⅓ cups chopped nuts
⅔ cup red maraschino cherries, chopped and
  drained

Preheat oven to 350°. Grease and lightly flour two 9x5x3-inch loaf pans. Cream together butter or margarine and sugar in mixing bowl; add eggs, one at a time, beating after each addition. Stir in applesauce and milk. Sift together flour, baking powder, soda and salt; add to creamed mixture and mix well. Add lemon rind, chopped nuts and cherries. Pour into prepared pans. Bake 1 hour. Remove from pans and cool on rack. Place bread on board and slice with electric knife.

*Celery Stuffed with Pimiento Cheese*
### ROLLED LAMB SHOULDER
*POTATOES CHANTILLY     SPICY CARROTS*
*Mint Jelly     Parker House Rolls*
### FILBERT CAKE
*Suggested Wine: Red Burgundy (Pinot Noir)     Coffee*

## ROLLED LAMB SHOULDER

Preheat oven to 300°. Season a 5- to 6-pound rolled lamb shoulder roast with salt and pepper. Place on rack in an open roasting pan. Do not add water.

Roast uncovered 3-3½ hours or until meat thermometer registers 175° for medium, 180° for well-done. Allow about 30 minutes per pound for medium; 35 minutes for well-done. Serve roast on heated platter. Let stand at least 10 minutes before carving. Slice with electric knife.

*Makes 6-8 servings.*

## POTATOES CHANTILLY

**4 cups mashed potatoes, seasoned with salt and pepper**
**½ cup heavy cream, whipped**
**¼ cup grated Parmesan cheese**

Preheat oven to 300°. Grease a 1½-quart casserole. Put mashed potatoes into casserole. Top with whipped cream. Sprinkle with grated cheese. Bake 30-35 minutes or until browned.

*Makes 6-8 servings.*

## SPICY CARROTS

**12-16 small whole carrots**
**2 tablespoons butter or margarine**
**¼ teaspoon pepper**
**1 teaspoon sugar**
**½ teaspoon nutmeg**
**2 teaspoons fresh lemon juice**

Wash and scrape carrots. Put in saucepan; cover and cook in 1 inch boiling salted water until tender. Drain, leaving carrots in saucepan. Add butter or margarine, pepper and sugar. Shake over low heat 3-4 minutes. Sprinkle with nutmeg and lemon juice.

*Makes 6-8 servings.*

## FILBERT CAKE

**1½ cups old-fashioned rolled oats**
**2 cups boiling water**
**1½ cups sugar**
**¾ cup firmly packed light brown sugar**
**⅔ cup vegetable oil**
**3 eggs**
**2 cups sifted all-purpose flour**
**1½ teaspoons baking soda**
**2 teaspoons salt**
**2 teaspoons cinnamon**
**1 cup chopped filberts**
**Coconut Filbert Frosting (below)**

Preheat oven to 325°. Grease a 13x9½x2-inch pan. Put oats in small bowl; add boiling water and let stand 10 minutes.

Combine sugars, oil and eggs thoroughly. Stir in oatmeal. Mix well. Sift flour, soda, salt and cinnamon together; add to oatmeal mixture. Stir in filberts. Spread in prepared pan. Bake 50-60 minutes or until done. Remove from pan; place cake on board. Immediately spread cake with frosting. Broil 2-4 minutes until lightly browned. Cut into squares with electric knife.

**Coconut Filbert Frosting:**

**¼ cup butter or margarine, softened**
**½ cup firmly packed light brown sugar**
**¼ cup evaporated milk**
**½ teaspoon vanilla**
**½ cup chopped filberts**
**½ cup flaked coconut**

Cream butter and brown sugar in mixing bowl. Add milk and vanilla, stirring until smooth. Add filberts and coconut. Mix well.

## ROTISSERIE PORK BUTT WITH MUSTARD SAUCE
## BROCCOLI WITH BUTTERED ALMONDS
### Shredded Romaine with Oil and Vinegar Dressing
### Muffins and Honey
## PEACH MERINGUE CAKE
### Coffee

### ROTISSERIE PORK BUTT WITH MUSTARD SAUCE

1 3-pound smoked pork butt
2-3 tablespoons dry mustard
2 tablespoons flour
3 tablespoons sugar
½ teaspoon salt
1 tablespoon vinegar
2 tablespoons dairy sour cream

Remove cloth wrapping from meat; tie with string for rotisserie broiling. Arrange meat evenly on spit, piercing through the center lengthwise. Place broiler pan on bottom of compartment and broil meat on low heat broiling position 1½ hours. Change to high heat broiling position and continue broiling 1 hour longer or until desired doneness.

Meanwhile, combine mustard, flour, sugar and salt in 1-quart saucepan; blend in ⅔ cup water, stirring to dissolve all lumps. Cook over medium heat, stirring constantly, until mixture thickens and boils. Remove from heat; stir in vinegar and sour cream. Slice pork with electric knife and serve with hot sauce.

*Makes 6-8 servings.*

### BROCCOLI WITH BUTTERED ALMONDS

2 bunches broccoli (each about 1 pound), cooked
6 tablespoons butter or margarine
¼ cup sliced blanched toasted almonds
⅛ teaspoon pepper

Arrange broccoli in a heated serving dish. Melt butter or margarine in saucepan and cook over medium heat until lightly browned. Add almonds and pepper. Stir to coat almonds. Pour over broccoli.

*Makes 6-8 servings.*

### PEACH MERINGUE CAKE

1¼ cups sifted cake flour
1¼ teaspoons baking powder
¾ teaspoon salt
½ cup butter or margarine
1½ cups sugar
4 eggs, separated
3 tablespoons milk
1 tablespoon vanilla
1 cup heavy cream, whipped
1 14-ounce package (1½ cups) frozen sliced peaches, thawed and drained

Preheat oven to 350°. Grease and lightly flour two 8-inch round layer cake pans. Sift together flour, baking powder and salt. Set aside. Cream butter or margarine in mixing bowl; add ½ cup of the sugar and egg yolks. Beat until fluffy. Add sifted dry ingredients; mix well. Add milk and vanilla; beat well. Spread batter in prepared pans. Beat egg whites until frothy; gradually add remaining sugar, beating well after each addition. Beat until stiff and glossy. Top each layer of batter with meringue. Bake 30-35 minutes. Remove from pans and cool thoroughly on rack. Just before serving, combine whipped cream and peaches. Use as filling and topping for cake layers. Cut cake into wedges with electric knife.

Mustard

*Pineapple Sticks and Apple Wedges with Salted Sour Cream*
## OVEN BARBECUED ROAST PORK
*Roast Potatoes      Corn Sticks*
## BRUSSELS SPROUTS WITH WALNUT BUTTER
## CHOCOLATE NUT ICE CREAM TORTE
*Suggested Wine: Rosé      Demitasse*

## OVEN BARBECUED ROAST PORK

1 6-pound pork loin roast
1 medium onion, chopped
⅓ cup chopped celery
¼ teaspoon garlic powder
2 tablespoons brown sugar
2 teaspoons prepared mustard
1 10½-ounce can condensed tomato soup
2 tablespoons Worcestershire sauce
2 tablespoons vinegar
**Dash Tabasco**
2 16-ounce cans small whole potatoes, drained
**Paprika**

Preheat oven to 350°. Place roast, fat side up, in shallow roasting pan. Roast uncovered 2 hours.

Combine remaining ingredients except potatoes and paprika in 1-quart saucepan; simmer 5 minutes. Drain fat from roasting pan; arrange potatoes on one side of pork and sprinkle with paprika. Spoon some of the tomato sauce over pork; continue roasting 1 hour or until meat thermometer registers 185°. Let roast stand at least 10 minutes before carving. Serve pork and potatoes on heated platter with remaining hot sauce. For carving instructions see page 20.
*Makes 6-8 servings.*

*The word Restaurant is believed to have originated in the mid XVIth Century when a medicinal soup served in a favorite tavern was called "Restorant." Soon the tavern took on the name of its famous soup and later on other taverns also became known by the name "Restorant."*

## BRUSSELS SPROUTS WITH WALNUT BUTTER

2 pounds fresh Brussels sprouts
⅛ teaspoon freshly ground black pepper
3 tablespoons butter or margarine
¼ cup chopped walnuts

Wash and trim Brussels sprouts. Soak 20 minutes in cold salted water. Drain. Cook Brussels sprouts in 1 inch boiling salted water, uncovered, 5 minutes. Cover and continue cooking over moderate heat 10-15 minutes or longer, until crisp-tender. Drain, if necessary. Season with pepper. Brown butter or margarine. Pour over Brussels sprouts. Sprinkle with nuts.
*Makes 6-8 servings.*

## CHOCOLATE NUT ICE CREAM TORTE

½ gallon chocolate ice cream, softened
1 cup crushed chocolate wafer cookies
1 cup miniature marshmallows
½ cup broken pecans
½ cup heavy cream, whipped
**Chocolate Sauce (below) or Blender Chocolate Sauce (page 71)**

Put softened ice cream in mixing bowl. Fold in crushed cookies, marshmallows and pecans. Pour into 7-cup mold. Freeze until firm.

To serve, unmold and garnish around base with whipped cream. Cut into wedges with electric knife and serve with Chocolate Sauce.

**Chocolate Sauce:**

1 6-ounce package (1 cup) semisweet chocolate pieces
½ cup heavy cream
½ teaspoon vanilla

Combine chocolate and cream in a saucepan and cook over low heat until chocolate melts. Stir in vanilla. Cool before serving.

*Cherry Tomatoes, Carrot and Green Pepper Strips*
*BEEF TONGUE WITH RAISIN SAUCE*
*Buttered Noodles or STUFFED BAKED POTATOES*
*French-style String Beans      Rolls*
*STRAWBERRY TREATS or Apple Pie*
*Suggested Wine: Claret (Grignolino)  or Cold Beer*

## BEEF TONGUE WITH RAISIN SAUCE

1 3- to 4-pound smoked beef tongue
1 stalk celery
2 bay leaves
1 large onion, quartered
Raisin Sauce (below)

Place meat, celery, bay leaves and onion in Dutch oven and add enough water to cover. Cover and cook over low heat, simmering 3-4 hours until meat is tender. Plunge tongue in cold water. Peel and chill. Slice and serve with Raisin Sauce. For carving instructions see page 22.
*Makes 10-12 servings.*

**Raisin Sauce:**

12 gingersnaps, crushed
1 cup firmly packed brown sugar
2½ cups water
½ cup vinegar
Juice of 2 lemons
½ cup seedless raisins

Put gingersnaps in saucepan. Add remaining ingredients and mix. Cook mixture over moderate heat 10-15 minutes until smooth.

## STUFFED BAKED POTATOES

6 large (about 4 pounds) long baking potatoes, washed and dried
1 whole egg, or 2 egg yolks, beaten
½ cup hot milk
¼ cup butter or margarine
1 teaspoon salt
¼ teaspoon pepper
2 tablespoons chopped fresh parsley

Preheat oven to 350°. Puncture potato skins with fork and bake 1¼ hours or until tender. With electric knife, cut each potato in half lengthwise. Scoop out, leaving shell intact. Mash potato; beat in egg and enough hot milk to make a smooth mixture. Add butter, salt, pepper and parsley. Beat until light. Fill potato shells lightly. Place potatoes in shallow pan. Increase oven heat to 450°. Return potatoes to oven and bake 15 minutes longer or until thoroughly heated and lightly browned on top.
*Makes 12 servings.*

## STRAWBERRY TREATS

2 cups sifted all-purpose flour
½ teaspoon salt
1 cup butter or margarine, softened
1 8-ounce package cream cheese, softened
Thick strawberry jam
Confectioners' sugar

Combine flour and salt in mixing bowl. Cut butter or margarine into dry ingredients with pastry blender or two knives. Blend in cream cheese. Chill thoroughly.

Preheat oven to 425°. Roll dough thin on lightly floured board; cut into 3-inch squares with electric knife. Place teaspoonful of jam in center of each square; bring two opposite corners together to form triangle and seal edges. Place on ungreased cooky sheets and bake 10-12 minutes. Sprinkle with confectioners' sugar while still warm. Serve with coffee or tea.
*Makes about 3 dozen.*

*Hot Cheese Appetizers*
### ROAST APPLE STUFFED SHOULDER OF PORK
*Buttered Corn*      BRAISED CELERY
*Croissants*      *Tomato Aspic Salad Mold*
BERRY CAKE *or Pound Cake with Sliced Strawberry Ice Cream*
*Suggested Wine: Red Burgundy (Pinot Noir)*      *Coffee*

## ROAST APPLE STUFFED SHOULDER OF PORK

1 5- to 6-pound pork shoulder, boned
Salt and pepper
5 slices bacon, cooked, drained and chopped
1½ cups bread crumbs
1½ cups cored pared chopped apples
1 tablespoon chopped parsley
1 tablespoon chopped onion
1 tablespoon chopped green pepper
⅛ teaspoon *each* marjoram, ground cloves, nutmeg
   and thyme
1 large bay leaf
1 large onion, chopped
1 stalk celery, diced
1½ cups cold water

Preheat oven to 450°. Sew edges of pork shoulder closed, leaving small opening in side for stuffing. Season meat with salt and pepper. Set aside.

Combine bacon, bread crumbs, apples, parsley, onion, green pepper, marjoram, cloves, nutmeg and thyme; mix well. Stuff pocket of meat with mixture and fasten with thread or skewers.

Place meat in uncovered roasting pan. Add bay leaf, onion, celery and cold water. Roast 25 minutes, turning meat frequently until brown and crisp. Reduce heat to 375° and continue roasting 2-2½ hours or until meat thermometer registers 185° (25-30 minutes per pound), basting frequently with pan juices until tender. Serve meat on heated platter; slice with electric knife.
*Makes 6-8 servings.*

### BRAISED CELERY

¼ cup butter or margarine
½ cup chicken or beef stock
2 large bunches celery, sliced (about 7 cups)
Salt and pepper

Place all ingredients in saucepan. Cover and simmer 20-25 minutes or until crisp-tender.
*Makes 8 servings.*

## BERRY CAKE

½ cup butter or margarine
½ cup sugar
3 eggs, separated
1 teaspoon lemon extract
1 cup sifted all-purpose flour
2 teaspoons baking powder
½ teaspoon salt
¼ cup milk
2 10-ounce packages (2 cups) frozen strawberries,
   thawed and drained
6 tablespoons sugar
1 cup heavy cream
3 tablespoons confectioners' sugar

Preheat oven to 350°. Grease two 8-inch round layer cake pans and line with waxed paper. Put butter or margarine in mixing bowl. Gradually add ½ cup sugar and cream thoroughly. Add egg yolks and lemon extract, beating until fluffy. Sift together flour, baking powder and salt. Add dry ingredients alternately with milk to creamed mixture. Mix only until combined. Pour into prepared pans; spread strawberries over batter.

Beat egg whites until stiff but not dry. Gradually add 6 tablespoons sugar, two tablespoons at a time. Beat until mixture is stiff and glossy. Spread meringue over berries. Bake 35-40 minutes. Cool 10 minutes in pans. Remove from pans and invert one layer on the other so rounded tops are together. Combine cream and confectioners' sugar; whip until stiff. Frost top and sides of cake. Place cake on board and cut into wedges with electric knife.

Marinated Artichoke Hearts
STUFFED VEAL ROLL
Buttered Noodles     Crescent Rolls
PEACH GELATIN SALAD MOLD
CHOCOLATE CREAM CAKE
Suggested Wine: Sauterne (Semillon)     Coffee

## STUFFED VEAL ROLL

6 sausages, cooked and sliced
2 cups canned applesauce
2 teaspoons instant minced onion
½ teaspoon salt
Dash pepper
1 cup hot consommé
1 cup seasoned bread crumbs
1 cup cracker crumbs
1 3- to 4-pound breast of veal, boned
Butter or margarine, softened

Preheat oven to 350°. Combine sausage, applesauce, onion, salt, pepper, consommé, bread crumbs and cracker crumbs in mixing bowl; mix well. Place meat on flat surface and spread stuffing over it. Roll up and tie securely; fasten ends with skewers and string. Rub entire meat roll with butter or margarine. Place in roasting pan; cover with heavy-duty foil and roast 1 hour. Remove foil and add 1 cup hot water to pan; replace foil. Roast 1½ hours longer or until meat is fork tender. Slice carefully with electric knife and serve.
*Makes 5-6 servings.*

## PEACH GELATIN SALAD MOLD

1 3-ounce package raspberry-flavored gelatin
1 cup boiling water
¾ cup cold water
1 1-pound can peach halves (reserve syrup)
1 3-ounce package orange-flavored gelatin
1 cup boiling water
1 3-ounce package cream cheese, softened
½ cup chopped walnuts
Head lettuce

Dissolve raspberry gelatin in 1 cup boiling water. Add cold water. Pour about half of the mixture into a 1½-quart ring mold. Chill until syrupy. Place peach halves, cut side up, in mold. Pour remaining raspberry gelatin over peaches. Chill until partially set.

Meanwhile, dissolve orange gelatin in 1 cup boiling water. Blend in cheese. If necessary, add water to reserved syrup to make ¾ cup; add to cheese mixture. Chill until very thick; whip until fluffy. Add walnuts. Spoon gently over set raspberry gelatin in mold. Chill until firm. To serve, unmold on bed of crisp lettuce leaves.
*Makes 10 servings.*

## CHOCOLATE CREAM CAKE

3 squares (3 ounces) unsweetened chocolate
2½ cups sifted cake flour
1 teaspoon salt
1 teaspoon baking soda
¾ cup shortening
1½ cups sugar
4 eggs
1 cup milk
Cocoa Butter Filling (below)
2 cups heavy cream, whipped and sweetened

Preheat oven to 350°. Grease and lightly flour two 9-inch round layer cake pans. Melt chocolate in saucepan; cool slightly. Sift together flour, salt and baking soda; set aside. Cream shortening and sugar in mixing bowl; beat in eggs, one at a time, until light and fluffy. Add flour mixture alternately with milk, beating well. Stir in chocolate. Pour batter into prepared pans. Bake 30-40 minutes. Remove from pans and cool on racks. Spread Cocoa Butter Filling between layers and frost top and sides of cake with whipped cream. Cut cake into individual servings with electric knife.

**Cocoa Butter Filling:**

1 cup butter or margarine, softened
¾ cup confectioners' sugar
½ cup unsweetened cocoa
1 teaspoon vanilla

Cream butter or margarine in small mixing bowl. Gradually beat in remaining ingredients until fluffy.

*Banana Chunks   Macadamia Nuts*
**POLYNESIAN PORK**
*Rice   Sesame Seed Rolls*
**HONOLULU SQUARES**   *Fresh Sliced Pineapple*
*Suggested Wine: Rosé   Tea*

## POLYNESIAN PORK

1 1-pound pork steak, 2 inches thick
1 teaspoon paprika
2 tablespoons hot shortening
3 tablespoons brown sugar
¼ cup instant dry milk
2 tablespoons cornstarch
½ teaspoon salt
1 13½-ounce can pineapple tidbits, well drained
  (reserve syrup)
⅓ cup vinegar
1 tablespoon soy sauce
1 teaspoon Worcestershire sauce
⅓ cup water
1 green pepper, cut into 2x⅛-inch strips
1 small onion, thinly sliced

With electric knife cut meat into 2x½-inch strips.*
Sprinkle pork with paprika. Brown well in hot shortening in a 10-inch skillet over medium heat. Cover
and cook about 3-5 minutes or until tender, stirring
occasionally. Drain off drippings. Push meat to one side
of skillet. Combine brown sugar, dry milk, cornstarch
and salt in a 1½-quart bowl. If necessary, add water
to reserved pineapple syrup to make ⅔ cup. Gradually
add syrup, vinegar, soy sauce, Worcestershire sauce
and water to dry ingredients and stir until smooth.
Pour into skillet. Cook over low heat until thick and
smooth, stirring constantly. Stir in green pepper,
onion and pineapple. Cover and simmer over very
low heat 8-10 minutes or until vegetables are tender
but crisp. Serve over hot rice.
*Makes 4-6 servings.*

*Meat is easier to cut if partially frozen.

## HONOLULU SQUARES

2 cups sifted cake flour
¼ teaspoon salt
¼ teaspoon baking soda
1¼ cups sugar
½ cup butter or margarine, melted
½ cup honey
1 teaspoon nutmeg
4 large egg whites
2 tablespoons milk
1¾ cups moist shredded coconut

Preheat oven to 350°. Grease two 8x8x2-inch pans
and line with waxed paper. Sift flour, salt, soda and
sugar together in mixing bowl. Add melted butter or
margarine, honey, nutmeg, egg whites and milk to
flour mixture. Mix well. Do not overbeat. Stir in coconut. Pour into prepared pans. Bake 35 minutes or until
top is firm when lightly touched. Turn cakes out on
wire racks. Remove waxed paper at once. Cool thoroughly. Place on board; cut each cake into 16 squares
with electric knife.
*Makes 32 squares.*

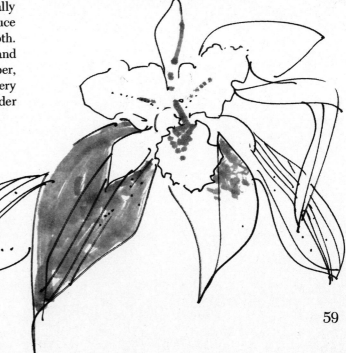

*Broiled or Batter-fried Shrimp     Soy Sauce Dip*
## SUKIYAKI
*Rice*

*TEMPLE COOKIES     Mandarin Oranges with Curaçao*

*Suggested Wine: Hot Sake     Tea*

## SUKIYAKI

1 pound beef tenderloin or sirloin
½ cup soy sauce
¾ cup canned chicken broth
3 tablespoons sugar
2 tablespoons vegetable oil
3 cups Chinese cabbage, cut into ½-inch diagonal slices (about ½ head)
12 scallions, cut into 2-inch lengths
2 medium Spanish onions, cut in half lengthwise, then into ¼-inch slices
3 large mushrooms, washed and sliced
4 stalks celery, sliced diagonally in thin strips
1 5-ounce can bamboo shoots
8 small cubes canned bean curd (optional)
1 cup canned shirataki (optional)
3 cups snipped fresh spinach (about ½ pound)

Slice meat very thinly with electric knife.° Set aside. Combine soy sauce, broth and sugar; mix well and set aside. Heat oil in heavy skillet. Add cabbage, scallions, onions, mushrooms, celery, bamboo shoots, bean curd and shirataki; pour soy sauce mixture over vegetables. Cook over high heat 8 minutes. Add spinach and meat; reduce heat and simmer 2 minutes. Push all solid ingredients down into sauce and cook 3 minutes longer. Serve with rice.

*Makes 6 servings.*

°Meat is easier to cut if partially frozen.

## TEMPLE COOKIES

2 cups sifted all-purpose flour
½ teaspoon baking soda
½ teaspoon cream of tartar
¼ teaspoon salt
½ cup butter or margarine
1 cup firmly packed brown sugar
1 egg
½ teaspoon vanilla
½ cup chopped peanuts

Preheat oven to 400°. Sift together flour, soda, cream of tartar and salt. In mixing bowl, cream butter or margarine until fluffy. Gradually add brown sugar, creaming until smooth. Add egg and vanilla. Beat well. Mix in flour mixture, a fourth at a time. Fold in peanuts. Shape dough into rolls; wrap in waxed paper. Chill until very firm. Place dough on board. With electric knife, slice ¼ inch thick and bake on ungreased cooky sheets 8-10 minutes.

*Makes 3 dozen.*

*Radish Roses, Celery Fans, Cheese Straws*
**BRAISED BEEF BURGUNDY**
*Noodles      French Bread      Pickled Beets and Onion Rings*
**APRICOT CAKE**
*or Brandied Peaches      Camembert Cheese and Crackers*
*Suggested Wine: Red Burgundy (Pinot Noir)      Demitasse*

## BRAISED BEEF BURGUNDY

3 pounds round steak
Flour
Salt and pepper
¼ cup butter
½ cup coarsely chopped onions
½ cup coarsely chopped leeks
½ cup coarsely chopped carrots
1 clove garlic, crushed
1 tablespoon *each* parsley and chives
2 tablespoons brandy
1 bouquet garni (page 82)
2 whole cloves
Dash crushed marjoram
8 crushed peppercorns
1 teaspoon salt
Red Burgundy wine

Preheat oven to 350°. With electric knife cut meat into 2-inch cubes.° Season flour with salt and pepper; dredge beef cubes. Melt butter in large skillet and sear meat over very high heat. Remove meat from skillet; place in 4-quart casserole. Reduce heat under skillet to low. Add onions, leeks, carrots, garlic, parsley and chives, stirring lightly to brown. Place brandy on a soup ladle, ignite and let flaming brandy drip over beef cubes in casserole. Add browned vegetable mixture to meat. Add bouquet garni, cloves, marjoram, crushed peppercorns and 1 teaspoon salt. Pour enough Burgundy wine over meat to cover. Cover tightly and bake 3¼ hours without opening lid.

To serve, remove bouquet garni and bring beef to the table in the casserole, or serve on a deep platter which has been heated and sprinkled with additional chopped parsley.
*Makes 5-6 servings.*

°Meat is easier to cut if partially frozen.

## APRICOT CAKE

1 cup dried apricots
1 cup water
½ cup shortening
1 cup sugar
1 egg
2 cups sifted all-purpose flour
1½ teaspoons baking powder
½ teaspoon baking soda
½ teaspoon salt
½ teaspoon cinnamon
1 6-ounce can evaporated milk
2 tablespoons lemon juice
Broiled Frosting (below)

Preheat oven to 350°. Grease a 9x9x2-inch pan. Place apricots and water in saucepan. Cover and cook over low heat, simmering 15-20 minutes until tender.

Force apricots through coarse sieve. (Or simmer apricots for 1-2 minutes. Place in blender container and run on speed 7 or high until smooth.) Cream shortening; add sugar gradually, beating until light and fluffy. Add egg; beat vigorously. Sift flour, baking powder, soda, salt and cinnamon together. Combine milk and lemon juice. Add sifted dry ingredients and the combined milk and lemon juice alternately to creamed mixture. Fold in apricot pulp. Pour into prepared pan. Bake 45-50 minutes or until done. Remove from pan; place on board.

Preheat broiler 5 minutes. Spread top of cake with Broiled Frosting. Place broiler pan (without rack) 5½ inches from heat. Place cake on broiler pan; broil 2 minutes or until frosting bubbles. Cut cake into individual servings with electric knife.

**Broiled Frosting:**

⅓ cup blanched almonds, slivered and toasted
3 tablespoons butter, melted
½ cup firmly packed brown sugar
2 tablespoons light cream

Combine all ingredients.

# Especially for
# ENTERTAINING

*Sliced Tomato and Egg in Chicken Aspic*
## POTTED VEAL WITH DUMPLINGS
*Broccoli or* GINGER GREEN BEANS
## PINEAPPLE UPSIDE-DOWN CAKE
*Coffee*

## POTTED VEAL WITH DUMPLINGS

2-pound veal shoulder
1 onion, thinly sliced
2 teaspoons salt
¼ teaspoon pepper
½ teaspoon Worcestershire sauce
2 cups diced raw potatoes
6 carrots, thinly sliced
¼ cup all-purpose flour
Dumplings (below)

With electric knife cut meat into 1-inch cubes.° Simmer veal and onion in 1 quart water for 1 hour. Add salt, pepper, Worcestershire sauce, potatoes and carrots. Continue cooking 15 minutes longer.

Blend together flour and ¼ cup cold water; add to pan juices and stir about 1 minute or until slightly thickened. Prepare Dumplings and drop by teaspoonfuls on top of meat. Cover tightly and steam 12 minutes.
*Makes 4-6 servings.*

°Meat is easier to cut if partially frozen.

Dumplings:

1½ cups all-purpose flour
3 teaspoons baking powder
¾ teaspoon salt
2 tablespoons shortening
¾ cup milk

Sift flour; sift again with baking powder and salt. Cut in shortening until mixture is crumbly. Add milk; mix to a soft dough.

## GINGER GREEN BEANS

2 tablespoons butter or margarine
½ teaspoon garlic salt
⅛ teaspoon ginger
1 3-ounce can sliced mushrooms
½ teaspoon salt
1 9-ounce package frozen cut green beans, cooked and drained
1 teaspoon cornstarch
1 tablespoon vinegar

Melt butter or margarine in saucepan; add garlic salt and cook 1 minute over medium heat. Add ginger, mushrooms, salt and cooked green beans. Bring to a boil. Cover and cook about 5 minutes. Blend cornstarch and vinegar; add to beans. Reduce heat to low and cook about 1 minute, stirring constantly, until sauce thickens.
*Makes 4 servings.*

## PINEAPPLE UPSIDE-DOWN CAKE

1 17-ounce package white cake mix
2 tablespoons butter
1 cup firmly packed brown sugar
9 canned pineapple rings
9 maraschino cherries

Preheat oven to 350°. Prepare cake mix as directed on package. Melt butter in 10-inch skillet over low heat. Add brown sugar; stir until melted. Remove from heat. Arrange pineapple and cherries on brown sugar in skillet. Pour cake batter on top. Place skillet in oven and bake 45-50 minutes or until top is firm when lightly touched. Loosen sides of cake with knife and invert cake directly onto serving plate or cutting board. With electric knife, cut cake into individual servings.

*Melon Balls in White Wine*
## STANDING RIB ROAST
*Lyonnaise Potatoes*     *Buttered Carrots*
*Hot Brioches*     *Butter Curls*     SPINACH SALAD MOLD
## ALMOND BUTTERSCOTCH TORTE
*Suggested Wine: Red Burgundy (Pinot Noir)*     *Demitasse*

### STANDING RIB ROAST

Preheat the oven to 325°. Place 5- to 7-pound standing rib roast (2 to 3 ribs), fat side up, on rack in open roasting pan. Sprinkle heavy layer of garlic salt over fat. Insert meat thermometer so the bulb reaches the center of thickest part, being sure it does not rest in fat or on bone. Do not add water. Roast uncovered. Meat thermometer will register 140° for rare; 160° for medium; 170° for well-done. Allow 23-25 minutes per pound for rare; 27-30 minutes for medium; 32-35 minutes for well-done. Let roast stand at least 10 minutes before carving. For carving instructions see page 18.
*Makes 6-8 servings.*

### SPINACH SALAD MOLD

**5 10-ounce packages frozen chopped spinach, thawed**
**1¾ cups dairy sour cream**
**½ cup finely chopped celery**
**6 tablespoons grated onion**
**2 tablespoons vinegar**
**1 tablespoon finely chopped parsley**
**1 tablespoon salt**
**½ teaspoon anise seed**
**1 unpared cucumber**
**Watercress**
**¼ cup grated carrot**

Oil a 6-cup ring mold. Simmer spinach 2-3 minutes in 1¼ cups unsalted water in large saucepan; rinse in cold water and drain thoroughly (use absorbent paper to assist in draining) and cool. Combine ¾ cup of the sour cream, celery, onion, vinegar, parsley, salt and anise seed in mixing bowl. Add spinach and mix well. Pack lightly into prepared mold; chill 2-3 hours.

Grate enough of cucumber to make 2 tablespoons. Combine with remaining sour cream; set aside. Score and slice remaining unpared cucumber. To serve, unmold on bed of watercress; garnish with cucumber slices sprinkled with grated carrot. Serve with sauce.
*Makes 6-8 servings.*

### ALMOND BUTTERSCOTCH TORTE

**6 eggs, separated**
**1½ cups sugar**
**1 teaspoon baking powder**
**2 teaspoons vanilla**
**1 teaspoon almond extract**
**2 cups graham cracker crumbs**
**1 cup finely chopped almonds**
**1 cup heavy cream, whipped and sweetened**
**Whole almonds**
**Butterscotch Sauce (below)**

Preheat oven to 325°. Line 9-inch springform pan with waxed paper. Beat egg yolks until thick and lemon colored. Beat in gradually ½ cup of the sugar, baking powder, vanilla and almond extract. Beat egg whites until soft peaks form; add remaining sugar, one tablespoonful at a time, and continue beating until stiff and glossy. Gently fold in egg yolks, crumbs and nuts. Pour into prepared pan. Bake 1 hour. Cool in pan on rack 10 minutes. Remove carefully from pan and place on serving dish. Peel off waxed paper and cool thoroughly. Just before serving, frost top of torte with whipped cream and garnish with whole almonds. Cut into wedges with electric knife and serve with Butterscotch Sauce.

**Butterscotch Sauce:**

**1 cup firmly packed brown sugar**
**1 tablespoon all-purpose flour**
**¼ cup orange juice**
**¼ cup water**
**¼ cup butter**
**2 eggs, beaten**
**½ teaspoon vanilla**

Combine sugar and flour in small saucepan. Blend in orange juice, water and butter. Cook over low heat, stirring constantly, until thickened. Slowly add a small amount of hot mixture to eggs, stirring constantly; return to saucepan and cook 1 minute longer. Remove from heat; add vanilla. Cool sauce before serving.

*BRAISED SPARERIBS WITH CORN STUFFING*
*ZIPPY BEETS*    Poppy Seed Rolls
*Onion and Cucumber Salad*
*PLUM PARTY MOLD*
*Suggested Wine: Claret (Cabernet)    Coffee*

## BRAISED SPARERIBS WITH CORN STUFFING

2 sections spareribs (each about 3 pounds)
½ lemon
½ teaspoon salt
¼ teaspoon freshly ground black pepper
⅛ teaspoon *each* ground cloves, nutmeg and thyme
1 large green pepper, seeded and finely chopped
1 extra large onion, finely chopped
2 tablespoons finely chopped parsley
1 clove garlic, finely chopped
2 stalks celery, finely chopped
1½ cups bread crumbs
⅛ teaspoon *each* sage and marjoram
Salt and pepper
2½ cups whole kernel corn
2 eggs
¼ cup milk
¾ cup white wine
¾ cup water

Preheat oven to 350°. Wipe sparerib sections with damp cloth, then with lemon. Combine seasonings; rub meat generously on both sides. Set aside.

Combine green pepper, onion, parsley, garlic, celery, crumbs, sage, marjoram, salt and pepper in mixing bowl. Add corn; mix well. Beat eggs and milk together; add to corn mixture. Mix well.

Place 1 sparerib section on rack in roasting pan; spread with stuffing. Cover with second sparerib section. Fasten sections together with skewers and string. Combine wine and water; pour over spareribs. Cover tightly and roast 3 hours or until meat is tender when pierced with a fork. Remove skewers before serving. If gravy is desired, strain pan juices into small saucepan. Bring to boil. Blend ½ cup *each* water and flour together. Stir into 2 cups pan broth until smooth. Pour gravy over spareribs or serve separately. Serve spareribs on heated platter. Allow two ribs for each serving, cutting all the way through with electric knife.
*Makes 6-8 servings.*

## ZIPPY BEETS

¼ cup butter or margarine
2 tablespoons cornstarch
2 tablespoons sugar
½ teaspoon salt
2 tablespoons grated lemon rind
¼ cup lemon juice
1⅓ cups water
¼ cup horseradish
3 pounds (about 16-20) small hot cooked beets, sliced

Melt butter or margarine in 4-quart saucepan; stir in combined cornstarch, sugar and salt. Cook about 1 minute over low heat, stirring constantly. Combine lemon rind, juice and water; gradually add to sauce. Cook, stirring constantly, until sauce thickens. Stir in horseradish. Add beets; heat thoroughly.
*Makes 6-8 servings.*

## PLUM PARTY MOLD

1 1-pound 14-ounce can (2 cups) purple plums (reserve syrup)
1 tablespoon cornstarch
1 tablespoon lemon juice
1 quart vanilla ice cream, softened

Pit and peel plums, then sieve into saucepan. Blend a few tablespoons syrup into cornstarch to make a smooth paste. Stir cornstarch mixture, remaining syrup and lemon juice into plums. Cook over low heat, stirring constantly, until thick and clear; chill. Pour ½ cup sauce into 7-cup mold; freeze until firm. Set aside ¼ cup sauce for garnish. Fill mold, alternating layers of ice cream and sauce; freeze until firm.

To serve, unmold on serving dish and spoon reserved sauce over mold. Slice with electric knife.
*Makes 8-10 servings.*

PLANKED STEAK
ASPARAGUS WITH CAPER BUTTER
*French Fried Onion Rings*
*Pickles     Hard Rolls*
POUND CAKE MELBA
*Coffee*

**...TEAK**

1-2 inches thick

...in center of broiler rack 3 inches from heat. Meanwhile, oil and heat wooden plank or heatproof platter. When steak is well browned on one side, season with salt, pepper and paprika. Turn to complete cooking on other side.

While steak is broiling, sauté mushroom caps in 2 tablespoons butter until brown. About 10 minutes before steak is done, transfer it to prepared plank or heatproof platter. (Steaks cut 1 inch thick require 20 minutes for rare and 25 minutes for medium. Steaks cut 2 inches thick require 35 minutes for rare and 40 minutes for medium.) Sprinkle tomato halves with cheese and top with bacon slices; arrange around steak alternately with mushroom caps and onions. Dot onions with 2 tablespoons butter.

Surround plank with a border of mashed potatoes and return to broiler 10 minutes longer or until tomatoes are cooked and potatoes and onions are browned. Garnish with parsley or watercress and serve immediately. For carving instructions see page 19.

*Makes 4 servings.*

## ASPARAGUS WITH CAPER BUTTER

2 pounds fresh asparagus, washed
2 teaspoons salt
⅛ teaspoon pepper
¼ cup melted butter or margarine
2 tablespoons capers

With electric knife cut off tough ends of spears. In 10-inch skillet, heat 4 cups water to boiling; add 1½ teaspoons salt. Add asparagus; cover and cook over low heat 12-15 minutes or until stalks are tender when pierced with a fork. Drain.

Combine ½ teaspoon salt, pepper and melted butter or margarine with capers; pour over asparagus and serve immediately.

*Makes 4-6 servings.*

## POUND CAKE MELBA

4 slices pound cake
4 slices vanilla ice cream
4 peach halves
Melba Sauce (below)

Place cake slice on each dessert plate. Top with ice cream slice and peach half. Pour 2 tablespoons Melba Sauce over each dessert.

*Makes 4 servings.*

**Melba Sauce:**

½ 10-ounce package frozen raspberries, thawed
¼ cup sugar
¼ cup currant jelly
¾ teaspoon cornstarch

Combine raspberries, sugar and jelly in saucepan. Bring to a boil. Dissolve cornstarch in 1½ teaspoons water and add to raspberries. Stir constantly over moderate heat about 1-2 minutes, until mixture thickens.

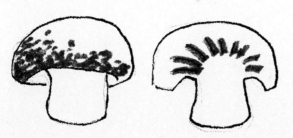

*Tomato Juice on the Rocks*
## CROWN ROAST OF PORK
*Spiced Apples*     *Baked Idaho Potatoes*     *Orange Buns*
*Green Beans Almondine*
## CHOCOLATE ICE CREAM ROLL
*Suggested Wine: Riesling*     *Coffee or Tea*

### CROWN ROAST OF PORK

1 10- to 12-rib crown roast of pork, trimmed and
 tied
⅓ cup butter
½ cup chopped onion
¼ cup chopped celery leaves
¼ cup finely chopped parsley
1 clove garlic, crushed
2 cups bread crumbs
½ teaspoon sage
Dash *each* thyme, savory, tarragon and nutmeg
2 cups sausage meat
Salt and pepper
Dash cayenne
¼ cup dry white wine
Watercress

Preheat oven to 350°. Melt butter in large skillet and
sauté onion 5-6 minutes until tender and transparent,
stirring constantly. Add celery, parsley and garlic;
cook and stir over low heat 1-2 minutes. Combine
bread crumbs, seasonings and sausage; add to onion
mixture. Season with salt, pepper and cayenne. Mix
well. Add wine, stirring constantly. Cool slightly; fill
pork roast with stuffing. Cover tip of each rib bone
with cube of raw potato to prevent burning. Place
roast on foil-covered rack in shallow pan and roast
until meat thermometer registers 170° (30-35 minutes
per pound). To serve, place roast on heated serving
platter; remove potato cubes and replace with paper
frills. Garnish with watercress. To carve, see instructions for crown roast of lamb on page 21.

*Makes 6-8 servings.*

### CHOCOLATE ICE CREAM ROLL

¾ cup sifted cake flour
⅓ cup unsweetened cocoa
¼ teaspoon salt
5 eggs, separated
1 cup sugar
1 tablespoon lemon juice
2 tablespoons unsweetened cocoa
1 quart vanilla ice cream, softened
Blender Chocolate Sauce (below) or
 Chocolate Sauce (page 51)

Preheat oven to 350°. Butter 15½x10½x1-inch jelly
roll pan and line with waxed paper. Set aside.

Sift flour, ⅓ cup cocoa and salt together twice. Beat
egg whites just until frothy; gradually add sugar, con-
tinuing to beat until stiff. Beat egg yolks and lemon
juice until thick and lemon colored. Fold into egg
whites. Fold in dry ingredients. Pour into pan. Bake
15-18 minutes.

Sift 2 tablespoons cocoa over a tea towel. Loosen
cake from sides of pan; invert on towel. Remove
waxed paper; trim away crusts. Roll cake up in towel;
cool on rack. Carefully unroll; remove towel. Spread
cake with ice cream; reroll. Freeze until firm. Slice
with electric knife and serve with chocolate sauce.

**Blender Chocolate Sauce:**

¾ cup hot milk or hot coffee
1 cup sugar
2 teaspoons vanilla
4 squares (4 ounces) unsweetened chocolate, cut up

Put ingredients in blender container; cover and run
on speed 7 (or high) until chocolate is liquefied. Serve
immediately as hot fudge sauce.

*Vegetable Juice with Lemon Slice    Melba Toast*
## ROLLED VEAL SHOULDER WITH PEACH GLAZE
*Oven-browned Potatoes    Poppy Seed Rolls*
*Asparagus Salad*    HERB DRESSING
*BANANA CAKE or Butterscotch Pie*
*Suggested Wine: Chablis (Pinot Chardonnay)    Coffee or Tea*

### ROLLED VEAL SHOULDER WITH PEACH GLAZE

1 3- to 4-pound rolled veal shoulder
1 12-ounce can peach nectar
2 tablespoons frozen grapefruit juice concentrate, thawed
½ cup firmly packed brown sugar

Preheat oven to 300°. Place roast on rack in open roasting pan. Do not add water. Roast uncovered 1½ hours.

Meanwhile, prepare glaze. Combine peach nectar, grapefruit juice concentrate and brown sugar in saucepan. Simmer 10 minutes. Cool. Remove veal from oven. Spoon one-third of the glaze over meat. Return to oven; continue roasting 20 minutes longer. Spoon another third of glaze over roast. Continue roasting another 20 minutes. Spoon remaining glaze over roast. Continue roasting until meat thermometer registers 170° (about 40 minutes per pound) or until tender. To serve, place rolled veal shoulder on heated platter; pour pan juices over meat. Slice with electric knife and serve.

*Makes 6-8 servings.*

### HERB DRESSING

1 tablespoon paprika
1 thin slice onion
¼ teaspoon tarragon leaves
¼ teaspoon chervil leaves
2 teaspoons capers
1 teaspoon fresh lemon juice
1 cup mayonnaise

Put all ingredients in blender container; cover and run on speed 4 (or high) just until capers are chopped. (Or finely chop onion and capers, and mix well.) Serve as dressing over chilled asparagus spears.

*Makes 1 cup.*

### BANANA CAKE

2¼ cups sifted cake flour
1 teaspoon baking powder
½ teaspoon baking soda
¾ teaspoon salt
½ cup shortening
1¼ cups sugar
2 eggs
1 teaspoon vanilla
¼ cup soured milk
1 cup mashed ripe bananas
Cream Filling (below)
Whipped cream

Preheat oven to 350°. Line the bottom of a 9x9x2-inch cake pan with waxed paper. Sift together flour, baking powder, soda and salt. In mixing bowl, cream shortening and sugar well. Add eggs and vanilla. Combine soured milk and bananas. Add sifted dry ingredients alternately with milk and bananas. Pour into prepared pan. Bake 40-45 minutes or until done. Cool. Remove from pan. With electric knife, split cake in half to make two layers. Spread Cream Filling between layers. Top with whipped cream; cut into squares.

Cream Filling:

2 cups milk
3 tablespoons *each* cornstarch and flour
¼ teaspoon salt
⅓ cup sugar
2 egg yolks, beaten
1 teaspoon vanilla
2 tablespoons butter or margarine

Scald 1½ cups of the milk in saucepan. Mix cornstarch, flour, salt and sugar; add remaining cold milk and make a smooth paste. Gradually add mixture to scalded milk, stirring constantly over low heat until thickened, about 5 minutes. Stir a small amount of hot mixture into beaten egg yolks; gradually add yolks to remaining mixture. Simmer and stir 3 minutes. Remove from heat; add vanilla and butter. Cool.

Apple-Cranberry Juice Cocktail

# ROAST RACK OF LAMB

*Potatoes Anna*    BAKED BANANAS    *Minted Peas*

*Hard Rolls*    *Marinated Mushroom and Escarole Salad*

## CHOCOLATE FROSTED RUM CAKE

*Suggested Wine: Red Burgundy or Zinfandel*    *Demitasse*

## ROAST RACK OF LAMB

1 teaspoon salt
¼ teaspoon pepper
1 teaspoon cinnamon
1 teaspoon ginger
2 3-pound racks of lamb
2 1-pound 14-ounce cans (4 cups) purple plums,
   drained (reserve 2 cups syrup)
12 whole cloves
Dash bitters

Preheat oven to 325°. Combine salt, pepper, cinnamon and ginger; mix well. Sprinkle half of cinnamon mixture over each rack of lamb. Place on rack in roasting pan. Roast uncovered 1¾ hours. Remove lamb and rack; drain excess fat. Return meat to pan. Add plums with reserved syrup, cloves and bitters. Return lamb to oven; roast 15-20 minutes longer, basting occasionally with pan juices, or until meat thermometer registers 175°. Serve lamb on heated serving platter encircled with plums. Pour pan juices over roast. To carve, see instructions for pork loin roast on page 20.
*Makes 8 servings.*

## BAKED BANANAS

3 large firm bananas, peeled
1½ tablespoons fresh lemon juice
3 tablespoons sugar
¼ teaspoon cinnamon
¼ teaspoon nutmeg
Dash ground cloves
½ teaspoon grated orange rind
¼ cup fresh orange juice
1 tablespoon butter or margarine

Preheat oven to 350°. Cut bananas in half crosswise with electric knife and then into lengthwise halves. Dip in lemon juice and place in shallow baking pan. Pour remaining lemon juice over bananas. Combine sugar, spices, orange rind and juice in small mixing bowl. Pour over bananas. Dot bananas with butter. Bake 20 minutes.
*Makes 6 servings.*

## CHOCOLATE FROSTED RUM CAKE

2 cups sifted cake flour
2 teaspoons baking powder
¼ teaspoon *each* baking soda and salt
½ cup butter or margarine
1 cup sugar
2 eggs, separated
1 teaspoon grated orange rind
½ cup orange juice
⅓ cup white rum
¼ teaspoon *each* almond extract and vanilla
Whipped Cream Filling (below)
Chocolate Frosting (below)
1½ cups chopped pecans

Preheat oven to 350°. Grease two 9-inch round layer cake pans. Sift together flour, baking powder, soda and salt. Cream butter or margarine; add ¾ cup of the sugar gradually. Add egg yolks and orange rind; beat thoroughly. Combine orange juice, rum, extract and vanilla; add alternately with dry ingredients to egg yolk mixture. Beat egg whites until stiff but not dry. Add remaining sugar gradually; beat thoroughly. Fold into batter. Pour into prepared pans. Bake 20-25 minutes. Cool. Remove cakes from pans and cool thoroughly on racks. Split each layer with electric knife. Fill all layers with Filling and frost cake with Frosting. Sprinkle nuts on top and sides of cake. Chill cake overnight. Cut into wedges.

**Whipped Cream Filling:**

2 teaspoons unflavored gelatin
2 tablespoons cold water
2 cups heavy cream
½ cup confectioners' sugar
⅓ cup white rum

Sprinkle gelatin over water in small saucepan; heat slowly until gelatin is dissolved. Cool slightly. Combine cream, sugar and rum; beat until stiff. Gradually add gelatin and beat just until it holds its shape. Chill.

**Chocolate Frosting:**

6 tablespoons butter or margarine
1 cup confectioners' sugar
2 eggs
4 squares (4 ounces) unsweetened chocolate, melted
2 tablespoons hot water

Cream butter or margarine in mixing bowl. Add sugar and beat thoroughly. Add eggs, one at a time. Blend in melted chocolate and hot water. Cool.

*Crabmeat Cocktail*
## ROAST DUCK WITH APPLE DRESSING
### POTATO PUFFS    ZUCCHINI CASSEROLE    *Pecan Muffins*
*Fruitcake or Coffee Rum Ice Cream*
*Suggested Wine: Claret (Cabernet) or Rosé    Coffee*

## ROAST DUCK WITH APPLE DRESSING

1 4- to 5-pound duck, oven-ready
1 teaspoon salt
3 cups bread crumbs
1 tablespoon diced onion
3 cups diced pared tart apples
½ teaspoon pepper
2 teaspoons poultry seasoning
1 tablespoon chopped parsley
1 teaspoon sage
Orange Sauce (below)

Preheat oven to 325°. Wash duck thoroughly and pat dry with absorbent paper. Rub cavity with salt. Combine remaining ingredients in mixing bowl; stuff cavity and close with skewers and string. Place on rack in shallow roasting pan. Roast 2-2½ hours (or 30 minutes per pound). Remove skewers and string. Place duck on heated serving platter and serve with Orange Sauce. For carving instructions see page 23.

*Makes 4 servings. (For 8 servings, use 2 ducks and double other ingredients.)*

Orange Sauce:

3 tablespoons butter or margarine
¼ cup all-purpose flour
1⅓ cups bouillon
1 teaspoon salt
¼ teaspoon paprika
1 tablespoon grated orange rind
⅔ cup hot orange juice
2 tablespoons dry sherry (optional)

Melt butter or margarine in saucepan. Stir in flour; cook over low heat until browned. Add bouillon and seasonings. Cook, stirring constantly, until thickened. Add rind, orange juice and sherry. Simmer 3 minutes.

## POTATO PUFFS

2 cups mashed potatoes
1 teaspoon salt
¼ teaspoon pepper
2 large eggs, beaten
1 teaspoon milk

Combine mashed potatoes, salt and pepper in mixing bowl. Beat until fluffy. Beat in eggs and milk. Drop mixture by rounded tablespoonfuls into deep fat, heated to 370°; fry until puffs are golden brown. Drain on absorbent paper.

*Makes 8 servings.*

## ZUCCHINI CASSEROLE

2 pounds zucchini
2 pounds (4 medium) tomatoes, peeled
½ cup dried onion flakes
1 teaspoon crushed oregano leaves
2 teaspoons salt
½ teaspoon pepper
½ teaspoon garlic powder
2 tablespoons vegetable oil

Preheat oven to 375°. With electric knife, slice zucchini and tomatoes ½ inch thick. Place half of zucchini on bottom of 10x6x2-inch casserole. Place half of tomatoes over zucchini. Sprinkle with onion flakes. Combine seasonings and sprinkle half of mixture over the zucchini and tomatoes. Top with remaining zucchini. Sprinkle with half of the remaining seasonings. Cover and bake 30 minutes. Remove cover and arrange remaining tomato slices over top. Brush tomatoes with oil and sprinkle with remaining seasonings. Bake uncovered 30 minutes longer.

*Makes 8 servings.*

## LOUISIANA BAKED STUFFED RED SNAPPER
### Lemon Wedges   Broccoli au Gratin   Onion Biscuits
### Tossed Green Salad   ROQUEFORT DRESSING
### NEW ORLEANS FRUIT TREAT
### Suggested Wine: Riesling   Coffee and Pralines

## LOUISIANA BAKED STUFFED RED SNAPPER

Salt and pepper
Nutmeg
1 5-pound snapper, cleaned and boned, with head removed
3 tablespoons butter
2 stalks celery, finely chopped
1 medium onion, finely chopped
¼ pound fresh mushrooms, washed and sliced
3 tablespoons finely chopped parsley
2 cups bread crumbs
½ cup milk, scalded
2 eggs, beaten
¼ cup butter, melted
½ cup hot water

Preheat oven to 350°. Combine ¼ teaspoon salt, ⅛ teaspoon pepper and dash nutmeg. Rub inside and outside of fish with mixture. Set aside.

Melt butter in skillet; sauté celery, onion and mushrooms. Add parsley and bread crumbs and cook over low heat 3 minutes longer, stirring constantly. Moisten with scalded milk; mix well. Remove from heat and cool slightly. Add eggs; season with ¼ teaspoon salt, ⅛ teaspoon pepper and dash nutmeg.

Fill cavity of fish with stuffing and fasten with skewers and thread. Put foil around neck of snapper to hold stuffing in place. Place fish in shallow baking pan. Bake 1 hour. Combine melted butter and hot water. Use to baste fish frequently. Serve on heated platter and cut into individual servings with electric knife.

*Makes 4-6 servings.*

## ROQUEFORT DRESSING

¾ cup vegetable oil
¼ cup vinegar
1 clove garlic
¼ teaspoon salt
Dash pepper
¼-¾ cup crumbled Roquefort cheese

Put all ingredients except cheese in blender container; cover and run on speed 4 (or high) about 30 seconds. (Or crush garlic clove and put all ingredients except cheese in covered jar; shake well.) Add crumbled Roquefort.

*Makes 1 cup.*

## NEW ORLEANS FRUIT TREAT

2 very large fresh pineapples
1 pint vanilla ice cream
1 cup heavy cream, whipped
3 tablespoons dark rum
½ teaspoon mace
¼ teaspoon ginger
½ cup chopped mangoes, bananas or peaches
½ cup diced orange sections
¼ cup sliced strawberries

Cut off pineapple tops and reserve. Scoop out inside of the pineapples, leaving a ½-inch shell. (Save and chop the scooped out portion to use in cream mixture.) Wrap pineapples in foil and place in freezer to chill.

The day before serving, soften ice cream; fold in whipped cream, rum, spices and fruits. Spoon into pineapple shells, filling above top to form mound; freeze until ready to serve. When serving, cover with the pineapple tops; with electric knife, cut each pineapple through center into thirds for individual portions.

*Makes 6 servings.*

*Chicken Liver Pâté with Toast Rounds*
*MUSHROOM STUFFED BEEF BIRDS*
*Parsley Spaghetti      Peas and Carrots*
*Dill Chips      Rye Rolls*
*CHERRY GLAZED ICE CREAM CAKE or Cherry Tartlets*
*Suggested Wine: Red Burgundy (Pinot Noir)      Coffee*

## MUSHROOM STUFFED BEEF BIRDS

1 round steak, ½ inch thick (2½ to 3 pounds)
½ pound fresh mushrooms
½ cup chopped parsley
½ cup chopped onion
1 cup grated sharp Cheddar cheese
¼ cup all-purpose flour
1 teaspoon salt
⅛ teaspoon pepper
3 tablespoons shortening or drippings
1 10½-ounce can condensed consommé
½ teaspoon dry mustard

Cut steak in six portions with electric knife. Pound steak to ¼-inch thickness. Remove mushroom caps from stems; chop stems and reserve caps. Combine mushroom stems, parsley, onion and cheese in mixing bowl. Place approximately 3 tablespoons mushroom mixture in center of each piece of steak, reserving remainder of mixture. Roll steak pieces around stuffing and fasten with skewers. Tie with string. Combine flour, salt and pepper. Dredge meat in seasoned flour. Brown in shortening or drippings in large skillet. Pour off drippings. Combine consommé and dry mustard; add to steak rolls. Add mushroom caps. Cover tightly and cook slowly over low heat 45 minutes. Add remaining mushroom mixture and continue cooking 45 minutes or until meat is tender. If gravy is desired, thicken pan juices with flour.
*Makes 6 servings.*

## CHERRY GLAZED ICE CREAM CAKE

Vanilla Wafer Crust (below)
1 quart vanilla ice cream, softened
½ cup sugar
3½ tablespoons cornstarch
¼ teaspoon salt
1 1-pound can (2 cups) red sour pitted cherries, drained (reserve liquid)
10-12 drops red food coloring
6 drops almond extract
1 tablespoon toasted sliced almonds
½ cup heavy cream, whipped and sweetened

Prepare crust. Spread ice cream in crust; freeze. Mix thoroughly sugar, cornstarch and salt in a saucepan. Gradually add reserved liquid. Cook, stirring constantly, until thick and clear. Stir in cherries, food coloring and extract; chill. To serve, lift cake from pan by foil extending over edges and gently remove foil from crust. Place cake on board and spread cherry mixture over ice cream; sprinkle with almonds. Cut into wedges with electric knife and serve immediately, topping each serving with spoonful of whipped cream.

**Vanilla Wafer Crust:**

Preheat oven to 350°. Line 8-inch round layer cake pan with heavy foil extending over edges. Combine 1½ cups vanilla wafer crumbs and ⅓ cup butter, melted; mix well. Press firmly against bottom and sides of pan. Bake 8-10 minutes. Cool.

*A Tumbler was originally a glass without a foot, made so that you could not set it down unless it was empty. If you did not drain your glass to the very end, whatever remained in it would tumble out.*

81

*CREAM OF CELERY SOUP*    *Bacon Wafers*
*ROAST LOIN OF PORK*
*Mashed Potatoes*    *Gravy*    *Cranberry Nut Muffins*
*BAKED FILLED TOMATOES*
*RED DEVIL'S FOOD CAKE*
*Suggested Wine: Rosé or Claret (Cabernet)*    *Coffee*

## CREAM OF CELERY SOUP

½ cup butter or margarine
4 cups thinly sliced celery
2 tablespoons finely chopped onion
½ cup all-purpose flour
4 cups chicken stock or 4 chicken bouillon cubes
 dissolved in 4 cups hot water
4 cups milk
½ cup finely chopped celery leaves
1 teaspoon salt
½ teaspoon pepper
Pimiento strips

Melt butter or margarine in a large saucepan. Add celery and onion and sauté 5 minutes or until celery is soft. Remove from heat. Stir in flour. Add stock and milk, stirring constantly. Stir and cook over low heat until soup thickens slightly. Stir in chopped celery leaves. Add salt and pepper. Serve hot, garnished with pimiento.

## ROAST LOIN OF PORK

1 5-pound center loin of pork
1 large onion, thinly sliced
1 clove garlic
Salt and pepper
1 cup all-purpose flour
2 small onions, finely chopped
1 small carrot, cut into small pieces
Bouquet garni (2 large bay leaves, 8 sprigs parsley,
 1 sprig thyme, 2 sprigs green celery leaves tied
 together with string)
1 cup hot water
3 tablespoons brown sugar
Watercress

Preheat oven to 350°. Have butcher separate the backbone from the ribs. Wipe meat with damp cloth. Insert onion slices in rib openings. Rub meat and fat with cut clove of garlic. Combine salt, pepper and flour and coat meat with mixture. Put chopped onion, carrot and bouquet garni in bottom of roasting pan. Pour hot water over vegetables. Place pork, fat side up, on rack in roasting pan and roast uncovered 2-2½ hours (30-35 minutes per pound), basting frequently with pan juices. Fifteen minutes before meat is done, remove from oven and increase heat to 400-425°; remove onions and carrots from meat. Sprinkle pork with brown sugar. Return meat to oven; roast 15 minutes longer.

If gravy is desired, strain pan juices into small saucepan. Blend in 1-2 tablespoons flour and cook over low heat until gravy thickens; serve separately. Serve roast on a heated platter; garnish with watercress. For carving instructions see page 20.
*Makes 6-8 servings.*

## BAKED FILLED TOMATOES

8 large tomatoes
2 10½-ounce cans condensed cream of mushroom
 soup
1 teaspoon salt
¼ teaspoon pepper
½ cup butter or margarine
2 onions, chopped
½ cup chopped celery
8 cups fresh bread crumbs
2 teaspoons poultry seasoning
½ teaspoon salt
⅛ teaspoon cayenne

Preheat oven to 375°. Wash tomatoes; with electric knife cut a thin slice from stem end of each. Scoop out centers. Chop and reserve center pulp. Pour soup into shallow 3-quart baking dish. Sprinkle inside of tomatoes with salt and pepper. Place upright in baking dish in soup. Melt butter or margarine in skillet. Add onion and celery. Cook 5 minutes. Add tomato pulp and cook 10 minutes longer. Add remaining ingredients; mix well. Fill tomatoes. Bake 30 minutes.
*Makes 8 servings.*

## RED DEVIL'S FOOD CAKE

2 cups sifted cake flour
½ cup unsweetened cocoa
½ teaspoon salt
½ cup shortening
1 cup sugar
½ cup firmly packed brown sugar
2 eggs
2 teaspoons baking soda
½ cup milk
1 cup boiling water
1 teaspoon vanilla
Vanilla Fluffy Frosting (right)

Preheat oven to 325°. Grease two 8-inch round layer cake pans. Combine and sift flour, cocoa and salt.

In a mixing bowl, cream shortening; add sugars. Beat until fluffy. Add eggs, one at a time, beating after each addition. Dissolve baking soda in milk. Add dry ingredients alternately with milk to batter; mix well. Add boiling water and vanilla. Beat until smooth. (Batter will be thin.) Pour batter into prepared pans. Bake 45-50 minutes. Remove from oven and cool in pans 10 minutes. Remove from pans and cool thoroughly on racks. Fill between layers and frost. Cut into wedges with electric knife and serve.

Vanilla Fluffy Frosting:

Cream ½ cup butter or margarine in mixing bowl; add 1½ cups confectioners' sugar and beat well. Add 1 egg and 1 teaspoon vanilla; combine. Add 1½ cups confectioners' sugar and beat until fluffy.

CREAM OF TOMATO SOUP     *Pretzels*
ROAST LEG OF LAMB
GLAZED ACORN SQUASH
*Herb Rolls     Minted Pear Salad*
COOKY CANDIES or *Vanilla Bavarian*
*Suggested Wine: Red Burgundy (Gamay)     Coffee*

## CREAM OF TOMATO SOUP

6 cups peeled chopped tomatoes
2 medium onions, diced
1 bay leaf
2 teaspoons salt
½ teaspoon pepper
¼ cup butter or margarine
¼ cup all-purpose flour
3 cups light cream

Combine tomatoes, onions, bay leaf, salt and pepper in saucepan. Simmer over low heat 20-25 minutes. Sieve. Melt butter or margarine in large saucepan; stir in flour. Add cream. Cook over low heat until thickened, stirring constantly. Slowly stir in tomato mixture. Simmer 10 minutes.

*Makes 6-8 servings.*

## ROAST LEG OF LAMB

1 5- to 6-pound leg of lamb
2 cloves garlic, slivered
Salt and pepper
Vegetable oil
Bouquet garni (page 82)
½ cup cold water
1 large onion, sliced
1 carrot, sliced

Preheat oven to 500°. Wipe lamb with damp cloth. Puncture meat in 6 or 8 places and insert garlic slivers. Place lamb in uncovered roasting pan and rub with salt and pepper; brush with oil. Sear meat in oven on all sides until nicely browned. Add bouquet garni, water, onion and carrot. Reduce heat to 350° and continue roasting about 2 hours (20 minutes per pound), basting frequently with the liquid in pan.

If gravy is desired, strain pan juices into small saucepan. Blend 1 teaspoon butter and 1 teaspoon flour together and add to pan juices. Cook over low heat, stirring constantly, until gravy thickens; serve separately. Serve lamb on heated platter. For carving instructions see page 21.

*Makes 6-8 servings.*

## GLAZED ACORN SQUASH

3 small acorn squash
½ cup firmly packed brown sugar
6 tablespoons butter or margarine

Preheat oven to 300°. With electric knife cut squash in half lengthwise. Scoop out seeds and fibers. Place, cut side down, in baking pan with ¼ inch water. Bake 1 hour. Turn squash right side up and sprinkle with brown sugar; dot with butter or margarine. Continue baking 30 minutes longer or until fork-tender.

*Makes 6 servings.*

## COOKY CANDIES

1 6-ounce package (1 cup) semisweet chocolate pieces
1 tablespoon shortening
1 cup finely chopped walnuts
⅓ cup sweetened condensed milk
1 teaspoon vanilla
¼ teaspoon salt
¼ cup soft butter or margarine
½ cup firmly packed brown sugar
1 egg yolk
½ teaspoon vanilla
1 cup sifted all-purpose flour
¾ teaspoon salt
¼ teaspoon baking powder

Melt chocolate pieces and shortening in top of double boiler over hot (not boiling) water. Remove from heat; mix in nuts. Add milk, vanilla and salt; combine thoroughly. Chill about 30 minutes or until firm enough to handle. Turn onto waxed paper and shape into a roll 12 inches long. Wrap and chill.

Cream together butter, brown sugar, egg yolk and vanilla in mixing bowl. Sift in flour, salt and baking powder; mix well. Form into a firm ball; roll out on waxed paper to 12x9-inch rectangle. Place roll of chocolate mixture along 12-inch edge. Roll up to cover filling. Wrap in waxed paper and chill until firm.

Preheat oven to 375°. Place dough on board. With electric knife cut dough into ½-inch slices. Place on ungreased cooky sheets and bake 10 minutes.

*Makes 2 dozen.*

# For
# HOLIDAYS
## and Special Occasions

*LONDON BROIL WITH BARBECUE SAUCE*
*Home-fried Potatoes    STUFFED ARTICHOKES*
*Fresh Vienna Bread*
*Fresh Fruit or Fruit Compote    Sugar Cookies*
*or Vanilla Ice Cream with Chocolate Sauce*
*Coffee*

## LONDON BROIL WITH BARBECUE SAUCE

Roll a 1½-pound flank steak in jelly roll fashion; secure at 1-inch intervals with skewers or toothpicks. With electric knife, cut steak crosswise into 6 slices, each 1 inch thick. Marinate in Barbecue Sauce (below) 4-5 hours or overnight.

Just before cooking, remove steaks from sauce; reserve sauce. Wrap 6 bacon slices around outer edges of steaks, securing bacon with toothpicks. Place steaks on grill about 5 inches from moderately hot coals. Cook 10 minutes until tender and browned on both sides, turning and basting frequently with reserved sauce. Remaining sauce may be served with steaks or stored in a covered jar in refrigerator for later use.

**Barbecue Sauce:**

2 tablespoons dried onion flakes
1 tablespoon brown sugar
1½ teaspoons salt
1 teaspoon dry mustard
¼ teaspoon pepper
½ cup fresh lemon juice
⅛ teaspoon garlic powder
1 teaspoon Tabasco
3 tablespoons vegetable oil
¼ cup catsup
¼ cup water
⅓ cup cider vinegar

Combine all ingredients in saucepan. Bring to a boil.

## STUFFED ARTICHOKES

6 medium-sized fresh artichokes
Juice of ½ lemon
½ pound ground beef
1 tablespoon butter or margarine
3 tablespoons grated Parmesan cheese
Béchamel Sauce (below)
1 large whole egg
1 large egg yolk
1 teaspoon salt
⅛ teaspoon pepper

Remove any coarse discolored outer leaves from artichokes. With electric knife, cut off each stem even with base of artichoke. Trim off thorny tips of leaves. Spread artichokes open by placing upside down on table and pressing the stem ends firmly. Gently pull out center cone of leaves; remove the fuzzy choke with a teaspoon. Let artichokes stand in water to cover with the lemon juice until ready to cook.

Brown meat in butter or margarine in skillet; remove from skillet and drain. Add cheese, Béchamel Sauce, eggs, salt and pepper. Mix well. Drain artichokes; fit them snugly in saucepan deep enough to cover tops of leaves. Spoon stuffing into centers of artichokes. Pour in enough water to half fill saucepan. Cover and cook over low heat 1 hour or until artichokes are tender.
*Makes 6 servings.*

**Béchamel Sauce:**

2 teaspoons butter or margarine
2 teaspoons all-purpose flour
⅓ cup chicken stock
3 tablespoons light cream
1 large egg yolk
Salt and pepper

Melt butter or margarine in small saucepan. Blend in flour. Remove from heat and slowly stir in chicken stock. Stir and cook about 1 minute until medium thick. Blend cream and egg yolk; add to sauce. Season with salt and pepper.

87

ROAST TURKEY
BREAD AND ONION STUFFING    Giblet Gravy
SWEET POTATO SOUFFLE    Croissants
CRANBERRY GELATIN MOLD
Mince Pie
Suggested Wine: Chablis (Pinot Chardonnay)
Coffee or Tea    Cognac

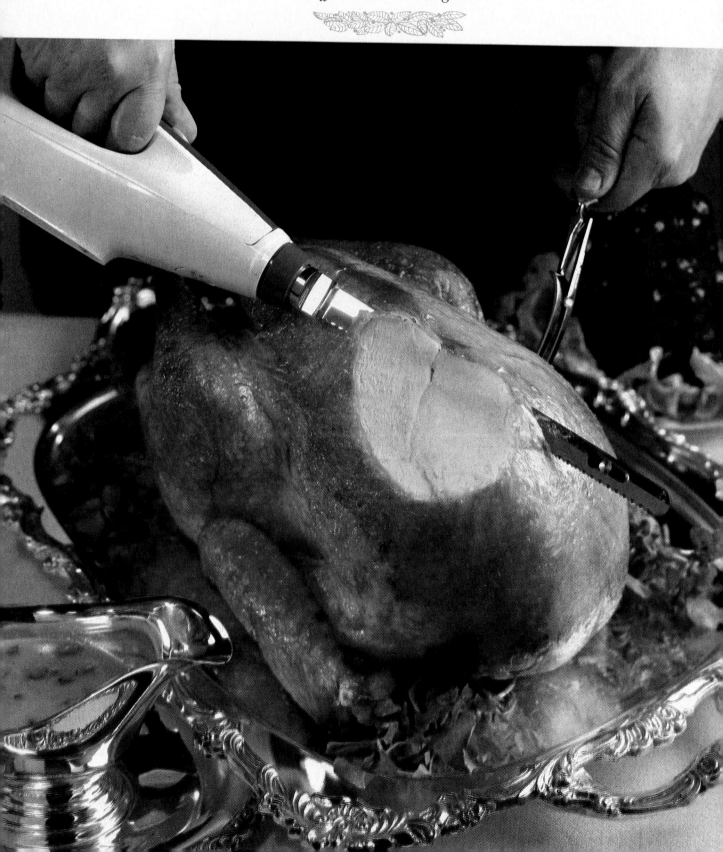

## ROAST TURKEY

Preheat oven according to chart below. Rub salt (⅛ teaspoon per pound) on inside of the body cavity. Fill cavity with Bread and Onion Stuffing (below) and close with skewers and string; truss. Place turkey on rack in shallow roasting pan. Cover with two thicknesses of cheesecloth dipped in vegetable oil. Follow chart below for approximate cooking time per pound. If more browning is desired, remove cloth the last 20-30 minutes of roasting. Remove skewers and string. Place turkey on heated platter and serve with gravy, if desired. For carving instructions see page 23.

| Oven-ready Weight | Oven Temperature | Approximate Minutes per pound |
| --- | --- | --- |
| 4-6 pounds | 325° | 30 |
| 6-8 pounds | 325° | 30 |
| 8-12 pounds | 325° | 20 |
| 12-18 pounds | 300° | 18 |
| 18-25 pounds | 300° | 15 |

**Bread and Onion Stuffing:**

12 cups bread crumbs
1 tablespoon salt
2 tablespoons poultry seasoning
¾ cup chopped parsley
¾ cup minced onion
1½ cups chopped celery
1 cup butter or margarine
2 eggs, slightly beaten

Mix bread crumbs, salt, poultry seasoning and parsley in mixing bowl. Sauté onion and celery in butter or margarine in skillet until golden brown. Add to bread crumb mixture. Add eggs and stir lightly.

*Makes 12 cups.*

**Variations:**

**Chestnut Stuffing**—Add 1 pound chestnuts, cooked and chopped. Mix well.
**Giblet Stuffing**—Add chopped cooked giblets. Mix well.
**Sausage Stuffing**—Crumble 1½ pounds sausage meat and brown over low heat; add to stuffing and mix well.

## SWEET POTATO SOUFFLE

2 cups cooked mashed sweet potatoes
¾ cup hot milk
3 tablespoons butter or margarine
¼ cup sugar
1 teaspoon lemon rind
½ teaspoon allspice
¼ teaspoon salt
⅛ teaspoon ground cloves
1 egg, separated

Preheat oven to 350°. Combine potatoes, milk, butter, 2 tablespoons of the sugar, lemon rind, allspice, salt and cloves in mixing bowl; mix well. Beat in egg yolk. Whip egg white until it stands in soft peaks. Gradually beat in remaining sugar; carefully fold into potato mixture. Turn into ungreased 1-quart casserole or souffle dish. Bake 1 hour or until firm in center.
*Makes 6-8 servings.*

## CRANBERRY GELATIN MOLD

2 envelopes unflavored gelatin
½ cup cold water
1 cup hot water
1 cup sugar
3 cups ground raw cranberries
½ cup chopped celery
½ cup diced apples
1 teaspoon grated orange rind
¼ cup fresh lemon juice
¼ teaspoon salt
½ cup chopped pecans or walnuts
Lettuce

Sprinkle gelatin over cold water. Add hot water and stir to dissolve gelatin. Add sugar; mix well. Put cranberries through food grinder, using fine blade, and add to gelatin. Add remaining ingredients. Pour into 5-cup ring mold which has been rinsed in cold water. Chill until gelatin is firm. Unmold on bed of crisp lettuce leaves.
*Makes 8 servings.*

*Shrimp Cocktail*
## ROLLED RIB ROAST
## SCALLOPED CORN AND TOMATOES
*Popovers     Watercress Salad*
## RUM FROSTED SPONGE CAKE
*or Sliced Oranges with Grand Marnier     Petits Fours*
*Suggested Wine: Sparkling Burgundy     Coffee*

## ROLLED RIB ROAST

Preheat the oven to 325°. Place a 5- to 7-pound rolled rib roast, fat side up, on rack in open roasting pan. Puncture fat in several places and insert garlic slivers; sprinkle with salt and pepper. Insert meat thermometer so the bulb reaches the center of thickest part, being sure it does not rest in fat. Do not add water. Roast uncovered. Meat thermometer will register 140° for rare; 160° for medium; 170° for well-done. Allow 32 minutes per pound for rare; 38 minutes per pound for medium; 48 minutes for well-done. Serve roast on heated platter. For carving instructions see page 18.
*Makes 8-10 servings.*

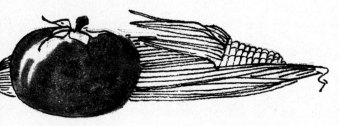

## SCALLOPED CORN AND TOMATOES

2½ cups whole kernel corn
4 medium tomatoes, sliced
½ cup chopped green pepper
2 tablespoons sugar
1 teaspoon salt
⅛ teaspoon pepper
1 medium onion, grated
⅓ cup bread crumbs
3 tablespoons butter or margarine, melted

Preheat oven to 350°. Grease a 2-quart casserole. Arrange alternate layers of corn, tomato slices and green pepper in prepared casserole. Add sugar, salt, pepper and onion. Combine bread crumbs and butter or margarine. Sprinkle over top. Cover. Bake 45-55 minutes or until done.
*Makes 6-8 servings.*

## RUM FROSTED SPONGE CAKE

1½ cups sifted cake flour
1 teaspoon baking powder
½ teaspoon salt
1½ cups sugar
6 eggs, separated
½ teaspoon cream of tartar
⅓ cup cold water
1 teaspoon lemon extract
1 teaspoon vanilla
**Rum Frosting (below)**

Preheat oven to 375°. Combine flour, baking powder, salt and 1 cup of the sugar; sift into mixing bowl. Beat egg whites and cream of tartar in another mixing bowl 1½ minutes or until soft peaks form. Slowly add remaining sugar and beat until stiff and glossy. Combine egg yolks, water, lemon extract and vanilla; add to flour mixture. Mix. Fold into beaten egg whites. Pour batter into ungreased 10-inch tube pan. Bake 40 minutes. Let cake hang upside down in pan on narrow-necked bottle until thoroughly cool. Remove from pan. Frost top and sides of cake with Rum Frosting. Cut into wedges with electric knife and serve.

**Rum Frosting:**

¾ cup evaporated milk, warmed
1 cup sugar
4 squares (4 ounces) unsweetened chocolate, shredded
1 teaspoon rum extract

Put all ingredients in blender container and run on speed 7 (or high) 3-4 minutes or until thickened. (Or beat until thickened.)

ROAST GOOSE
APPLE AND SWEET POTATO PUFFS
BRUSSELS SPROUTS WITH BUTTERED CHESTNUTS
Currant Jelly     Crescent Rolls
Plum Pudding with Hard Sauce
Suggested Wine: Red Burgundy     Coffee     Chartreuse Liqueur

## ROAST GOOSE

1 12- to 14-pound goose, oven-ready
1 lemon, quartered
1 tablespoon salt
¼ teaspoon pepper
4 large apples, quartered
4 cups prunes, pitted
4 whole red apples

Preheat oven to 450°. Rub goose inside and out with lemon. Combine salt and pepper and rub skin and cavity of goose. Stuff cavity with alternate spoonfuls of quartered apples and prunes. Fasten cavity of goose with skewers and string; truss. Place in shallow roasting pan. Prick skin of goose with tines of a sharp fork. Roast goose, uncovered, 20 minutes. Reduce heat to 350° and roast 1 hour longer. Remove goose from oven; baste with 1 cup boiling water. Return to oven and continue roasting 2 hours longer, basting every half hour with an additional ½ cup boiling water. (Allow a total cooking time of 15 minutes per pound.)

Prick whole apples with sharp fork and place in roasting pan during last 40 minutes of cooking time. Remove goose to heated serving platter; garnish with apples or spiced apples if desired. For carving instructions see page 23.

*Makes 8-10 servings.*

*In the XVth Century, wine jug stoppers were made in the shape of a man's head and the headgear denoted the quality of the wine. The best wine had a king's crown and the poorest had no hat at all.*

## APPLE AND SWEET POTATO PUFFS

2 pounds (4 large) sweet potatoes, cooked and mashed
1 large apple, pared, cored and shredded
½ teaspoon salt
1 teaspoon grated orange rind
⅛ teaspoon ground white pepper
¼ teaspoon allspice
1 large egg, lightly beaten
1 tablespoon butter or margarine
⅔ cup slivered blanched almonds
2 tablespoons butter or margarine, melted

Preheat oven to 375°. Lightly grease a cooky sheet. In mixing bowl, combine hot mashed potatoes with shredded apple. Add salt, orange rind, pepper, allspice, egg and 1 tablespoon butter or margarine. Shape into 2-inch balls using an ice cream scoop, if possible. Place on prepared cooky sheet. Sprinkle with almonds. Brush with 2 tablespoons melted butter or margarine. Bake 40-45 minutes. Serve hot.

*Makes 12 puffs.*

## BRUSSELS SPROUTS WITH BUTTERED CHESTNUTS

2 pounds fresh Brussels sprouts, washed and trimmed
Chicken stock
½ teaspoon salt
1 tablespoon finely chopped onion
¼ cup butter or margarine
⅔ cup cooked sliced chestnuts

Place Brussels sprouts in saucepan with 1 inch chicken stock, salt and onion. Bring to a boil and cook 5 minutes. Cover and cook 10-12 minutes longer or until Brussels sprouts are crisp-tender. Drain if necessary. Melt butter or margarine in small saucepan; add chestnuts and cook over medium heat until butter is browned. Stir to coat chestnuts. Pour over Brussels sprouts and toss lightly.

*Makes 6-8 servings.*

*Half Grapefruit with Maraschino Cherry*
## CROWN ROAST OF LAMB
*Mint Jelly     Parsley Potatoes     BROCCOLI HOLLANDAISE*
*Clover-leaf Rolls     Beet Salad on Shredded Greens*
## STRAWBERRY BAKED ALASKA
*Suggested Wine: Red Burgundy (Pinot Noir)     Demitasse*

## CROWN ROAST OF LAMB

1½ pounds ground lamb
1 cup chopped onion
3 cups cooked wild rice
½ pound fresh mushrooms, washed and sliced
½ cup chopped parsley
1 teaspoon salt
Dash pepper
1 7-pound crown roast of lamb, trimmed and tied

Preheat oven to 325°. Sauté ground lamb and onion in large skillet until onion is crisp-tender. Combine with rice, mushrooms, parsley, salt and pepper. Place lamb on foil-covered rack in shallow roasting pan. Fill center of roast with rice stuffing. Cover tip of each rib bone with cube of raw potato to prevent burning. Bake uncovered 2½ hours or until meat thermometer registers 175° (30-35 minutes per pound). To serve, place roast on heated platter; remove potato cubes and replace with paper frills. Garnish with watercress and raw mushroom slices, if desired. For carving instructions see page 21.

*Makes 12 servings.*

## BROCCOLI HOLLANDAISE

With electric knife, cut small piece off the ends of 3½ to 4 pounds of fresh broccoli. Split each large stalk lengthwise into halves or quarters. Then make lengthwise gashes in stalks so broccoli stalks cook as quickly as buds. Put in saucepan with 2 inches boiling water and 2 teaspoons salt. Boil 5 minutes uncovered. Cover; boil 10-15 minutes or until crisp-tender. Remove to serving dish and serve with Hollandaise Sauce (below) or Blender Hollandaise (below).
*Makes 8-10 servings.*

**Hollandaise Sauce:**

1½ cups butter or margarine
5 teaspoons fresh lemon juice
6 large egg yolks, well beaten
⅛ teaspoon *each* salt and cayenne

Divide butter into three pieces. Put one piece in top of small double boiler with lemon juice and egg yolks. Place over hot (not boiling) water and cook slowly, beating constantly with wire whisk or beater. Add second piece of butter when first has melted. Beat and cook until mixture begins to thicken. Add third piece of butter. Stir and cook until sauce is about as thick as mayonnaise, beating constantly. Remove from water immediately; add salt and cayenne.

**Blender Hollandaise Sauce:**

1 pound butter or margarine
4 egg yolks
3 tablespoons boiling water
2 tablespoons lemon juice
Dash white pepper
½ teaspoon prepared mustard

Melt butter in top of double boiler. When melted, pour off top portion; set aside. Discard remaining sediment in bottom of pan. Place egg yolks in blender container; cover and run on speed 1 (or low) slowly adding boiling water through center cap. Turn to speed 3 (or low) and add butter through center cap. Add lemon juice, white pepper and mustard just until mixed.

94

## STRAWBERRY BAKED ALASKA

1 package white cake mix
1 1-pound package frozen whole strawberries
1 quart strawberry ice cream, softened
6 egg whites
¾ cup sugar

Preheat oven to 350°. Grease and flour 9-inch spring-form pan. Prepare cake mix as directed on package. Bake in prepared pan 50-60 minutes, or until cake springs back when lightly touched. Cool in pan 10 minutes. Turn out on rack and cool thoroughly. Chill.

Barely thaw strawberries and drain if necessary. Arrange berries on cake to within ½ inch of edges. Spoon ice cream over berries. Freeze until very firm. Beat egg whites until frothy. Add sugar, one tablespoon at a time, beating well after each addition. Continue beating until meringue is glossy and stiff peaks form.

A couple of hours before serving, remove cake from freezer. Quickly spread meringue over entire cake. Return to freezer. Just before serving, bake at 500° for 4-5 minutes or until meringue is golden brown. Or store in freezer during dinner until ready to serve. Cut into individual servings with electric knife.

GLAZED BAKED HAM
ONION CASSEROLE
*Baked Yams or Hubbard Squash*
*Cheese Biscuits     Grapefruit and Avocado Salad*
DEVIL'S FOOD COCONUT LAYER CAKE
*Suggested Wine: Chablis (Pinot Chardonnay)     Coffee*

## GLAZED BAKED HAM

Preheat oven to 300°. Place a 12- to 14-pound smoked ham, fat side up, on rack in open roasting pan. Insert meat thermometer so the bulb reaches center of the thickest part. Be careful bulb does not rest in fat or on bone. Do not add water. Roast uncovered 3½-4½ hours or until meat thermometer registers 160° (or 18-20 minutes per pound). About 20-30 minutes before ham is done, spread with Peach Glaze (below). Return to oven to finish cooking and set glaze. For carving instructions see page 20.
*Makes 25-30 servings.*

### Peach Glaze:

1 cup peach preserves
1 tablespoon lemon juice
½ teaspoon ginger

Combine preserves, lemon juice and ginger. Mix well.

## ONION CASSEROLE

2 cups boiling water
1 teaspoon salt
2 pounds small white onions, peeled
3 cups cooked peas
2 10½-ounce cans condensed cream of mushroom
   soup
6 tablespoons chopped pimiento

Preheat oven to 350°. Grease 3-quart baking dish. Combine water, salt and onions in saucepan. Cook 25 minutes. Drain, reserving ¼ cup of the liquid. Combine onions and peas. Place in prepared baking dish. Combine soup and reserved onion liquid. Add pimiento. Toss with vegetables. Bake 25 minutes.
*Makes 12-14 servings.*

## DEVIL'S FOOD COCONUT LAYER CAKE

3 eggs
1½ cups sugar
¾ cup melted shortening
1½ teaspoons vanilla
3 squares (3 ounces) unsweetened chocolate
1½ cups sifted all-purpose flour
¾ teaspoon baking soda
¾ cup milk
Frosting (below)
Flaked coconut

Preheat oven to 350°. Grease and flour two 9-inch round layer cake pans. Beat eggs; add sugar and blend. Add melted shortening and vanilla. Melt chocolate over hot water; add to egg mixture. Sift together flour and baking soda; add alternately with milk to chocolate mixture. Bake in prepared pans 30-35 minutes. Remove from oven and cool in pans 10 minutes. Remove from pans and cool thoroughly on racks. Fill between layers and frost. Sprinkle cake with flaked coconut. Cut into wedges with electric knife and serve.

### Frosting:

2 egg whites
1½ cups sugar
5 tablespoons cold water
¼ teaspoon cream of tartar
1 teaspoon vanilla
¼ teaspoon salt

Put egg whites, sugar, water and cream of tartar in top of double boiler. Cook over rapidly boiling water, beating constantly, for 7 minutes or until frosting holds its shape. Remove from heat; add vanilla and salt.

*Lobster Bisque*
## STUFFED FLANK STEAKS
## ASPARAGUS WITH SOUR CREAM
*Garlic French Bread     Caesar Salad*
## APPLESAUCE CAKE
*Suggested Wine: Chianti     Coffee     Brandy*

### STUFFED FLANK STEAKS

2 2-pound flank steaks, each 10x6 inches
4 cups dry bread cubes
3 tablespoons chopped onion
1 teaspoon salt
¼ teaspoon *each* pepper and poultry seasoning
⅓ cup butter or margarine, melted
½ cup water
¼ cup hot vegetable oil
1 beef bouillon cube
½ cup hot water
Parsley
1 15½-ounce can small white onions

Score flank steaks diagonally. Combine bread, onion and seasonings in mixing bowl. Add butter and ½ cup water. Toss gently to mix. Heap bread mixture lengthwise down center of steaks. Fold in edges of steaks and close with skewers and string. Brown steaks in hot oil in 10-inch skillet over low heat. Dissolve bouillon cube in ½ cup hot water; pour over steaks. Cover and cook over low heat about 1½ hours or until steaks are tender. Garnish with parsley and small white onions. Slice with electric knife.
*Makes 8-10 servings.*

### ASPARAGUS WITH SOUR CREAM

6 tablespoons finely chopped onion
2 tablespoons butter or margarine
2 cups dairy sour cream
⅔ cup mayonnaise
2 tablespoons fresh lemon juice
½ teaspoon salt
¼ teaspoon ground white pepper
4 pounds fresh asparagus, cooked

Sauté onion in butter or margarine in skillet. Stir in sour cream, mayonnaise and lemon juice. Heat only until hot; do not boil. Season with salt and white pepper. Serve over asparagus. Garnish with paprika.
*Makes 8-10 servings.*

### APPLESAUCE CAKE

½ cup shortening
¾ cup firmly packed brown sugar
2 eggs
1 cup nuts, chopped
2 cups raisins
½ cup chopped citron
3 cups sifted all-purpose flour
3 teaspoons baking powder
1 teaspoon baking soda
¼ teaspoon salt
2 teaspoons cinnamon
1 teaspoon ground cloves
1 1-pound 4-ounce can (2½ cups) applesauce

Preheat oven to 350°. Grease 9-inch tube pan. Cream shortening in mixing bowl. Add brown sugar gradually, beating until light and fluffy. Add eggs, one at a time, beating vigorously after each addition. Coat nuts, raisins and citron with ½ cup of the flour; set aside. Sift together remaining dry ingredients; add alternately to egg mixture with applesauce. Fold in nut mixture. Bake in prepared pan 1½ hours. Cool in pan. Remove from pan and cool thoroughly on rack. Place cake on board and cut into individual servings with electric knife.

Great for
**OUTDOORS**

*Sliced Salami, Ham, Swiss Cheese*

*Split Seeded Hard Rolls*

*Sliced Bread*

*(White, Whole Wheat, Rye, Pumpernickel)*

*Sliced Eggs, Sliced Tomatoes, Anchovies*

*POTATO SALAD     COLESLAW*

*Green Pepper Rings, Red Onion Rings*

*Dill Pickles, Olives, Carrot and Celery Sticks*

*Jars of Mayonnaise and Mustard*

*Salt and Pepper*

*Fresh Pineapple Sticks*

*ALMOND COCONUT BARS*

*Suggested Wine: Rosé     Cold Beer*

*Coffee in thermos*

## COLESLAW

1 large head cabbage
½ cup mayonnaise
2 tablespoons vinegar
1 tablespoon grated onion
½ teaspoon celery seed
1 teaspoon sugar
½ teaspoon salt
⅛ teaspoon pepper

With electric knife, shred cabbage (about 4 cups) and place in deep mixing bowl. Combine remaining ingredients and mix with cabbage. Toss until well mixed. *Makes 8 servings.*

## POTATO SALAD

5 large potatoes, cooked and pared
½ teaspoon celery seed
1 teaspoon salt
Pepper
½ cup chopped green onions
1½ cups thinly sliced celery
½ cup sweet pickle relish
4 hard-cooked eggs, diced
1 cup mayonnaise
1 tablespoon prepared mustard
3 tablespoons vinegar
Salad greens

With electric knife, dice potatoes and place in large mixing bowl. Add celery seed, salt, pepper, onions, celery, pickle relish and eggs; toss lightly. In small bowl blend mayonnaise, mustard and vinegar. Add half of the mayonnaise mixture to potato mixture; toss lightly until potatoes are well coated. Cover and chill thoroughly. Add remaining mayonnaise mixture; toss again. Serve on crisp salad greens. *Makes 8 servings.*

## ALMOND COCONUT BARS

1 cup sifted all-purpose flour
1 teaspoon baking powder
¼ teaspoon salt
¼ cup butter or margarine
1 cup firmly packed light brown sugar
1 egg
1 teaspoon almond extract
1 cup shredded coconut

Preheat oven to 350°. Grease and lightly flour 8x8x2-inch pan. Sift together flour, baking powder and salt. Set aside. Melt butter or margarine in a large saucepan. Stir in brown sugar. Lightly beat in egg and almond extract. Mix coconut with dry ingredients and gradually add to butter-sugar mixture. (Batter will be stiff.) Spread in prepared pan. Bake 35 minutes or until brown. Cool 10 minutes in pan; remove from pan and cool on wire rack. Place cake on board and cut into 24 bars with electric knife. Store bars overnight in tightly covered container. *Makes 24 bars.*

Antipasto
PORTERHOUSE STEAK
Baked Potatoes     Italian Bread with Herb Butter
STRING BEAN SALAD or Tomato Halves
FRUITED RUM BARS
Cold Beer

## PORTERHOUSE STEAK

Place a 2½- to 3-pound porterhouse steak (1 to 2 inches thick) on grill so that 1-inch steak is 2-3 inches from the coals or 2-inch steak is 3-5 inches from coals. When one side of steak is browned, season with salt and pepper; turn and finish cooking on the second side. Season again.

Steaks cut 1 inch thick require a total cooking time of 18-20 minutes for rare and 20-25 minutes for medium. Steaks cut 2 inches thick require 30-40 minutes for rare and 35-45 minutes for medium. Place steak on board; for carving instructions see page 19.

*Makes 4-6 servings.*

## STRING BEAN SALAD

**3 cups cooked fresh string beans, chilled**
**¼ cup small white onion rings**
**¼ cup of the Dressing (below)**
**¾ teaspoon salt**
**¾ cup diced celery**
**½ cup diced green pepper**
**2 tablespoons pickle relish**
**Head lettuce**
**Tomato wedges**

Combine beans, onion rings, Dressing and salt in a mixing bowl; toss lightly. Cover and marinate 1 hour. Just before serving, add celery, green pepper and pickle relish. Toss lightly and serve in lettuce cups. Garnish with fresh tomato wedges.

*Makes 6 servings.*

**Dressing:**

**1 clove garlic, quartered**
**½ teaspoon salt**
**¼ teaspoon pepper**
**1 teaspoon chili powder**
**½ cup vegetable oil**
**3 tablespoons cider vinegar**
**2 tablespoons fresh lemon juice**

Combine garlic, salt, pepper, chili powder and oil. Let stand 1 hour. Remove and discard garlic. Add vinegar and lemon juice. Beat to mix. Store and chill in a covered jar in refrigerator until ready to use.

## FRUITED RUM BARS

**1½ cups sifted all-purpose flour**
**1 teaspoon baking powder**
**¼ teaspoon salt**
**2 teaspoons vanilla**
**½ cup shortening**
**½ cup sugar**
**2 eggs**
**¼ cup chopped glazed cherries**
**¼ cup chopped candied pineapple**
**¼ cup chopped raisins**
**¼ cup chopped citron**
**Rum Glaze (below)**

Preheat oven to 325°. Line 9x9x2-inch pan with waxed paper and grease paper lightly. Sift flour, baking powder and salt together. Cream together vanilla, shortening and sugar. Beat in eggs. Stir in flour mixture. Add fruit and mix well. Spread batter evenly over bottom of prepared pan. Bake 25-30 minutes or until lightly browned. Turn out on rack. Brush cake thinly with Rum Glaze while still warm. Cool. Place on board and cut in 24 bars with electric knife. Store in tightly covered jar or box.

*Makes 24 bars.*

**Rum Glaze:**

Blend together ¼ cup sifted confectioners' sugar, 1 teaspoon water and ½ teaspoon rum extract until smooth.

*Pineapple Chunks with Cheese Dip*
## BONED ROAST LAMB WITH PORK
*Rice with Mushrooms and Parsley*
*French Bread*    SPINACH SALAD
*PECAN ICE CREAM TORTE*
*Suggested Wine: Rosé     Iced Tea*

## BONED ROAST LAMB WITH PORK

1 6- to 8-pound leg of lamb
1 pork tenderloin
1 teaspoon marjoram, rosemary or thyme
Salt and pepper

Have butcher bone leg of lamb, replacing bone with pork tenderloin. Roll and tie roast for pan roasting or rotisserie; rub lamb with seasonings.

For pan roasting, preheat oven to 325°. Place lamb on rack in roasting pan and roast, uncovered, about 3 hours (30 minutes per pound) or until meat thermometer registers 185°.

For rotisserie, arrange lamb on spit, piercing roast through the center lengthwise. Cook over low coals 3-3½ hours or until meat thermometer registers 185°.

Place lamb on board or heated platter. Slice with electric knife and serve.

*Makes 8-10 servings.*

## SPINACH SALAD

1 pound spinach
1 clove garlic
½ cup vegetable oil
¼ cup red wine vinegar
¼ cup lemon juice
¼ teaspoon salt
Dash pepper
2 tablespoons Parmesan cheese
½ cup croutons
2 hard-cooked eggs, sliced
6 bacon slices, cooked and crumbled

Wash spinach; discard stems. Tear leaves into bite-size pieces. Chill 2 hours. Combine garlic and oil in glass jar; cover and let stand 1 hour. Discard garlic. Combine vinegar, lemon juice, salt, pepper and cheese in small bowl. Gradually beat in garlic oil, pouring in a thin stream. Pour dressing over spinach. Add croutons. Toss well. Garnish with egg slices and bacon.

*Makes 6-8 servings.*

## PECAN ICE CREAM TORTE

1 egg white
¼ teaspoon salt
¼ cup sifted confectioners' sugar
1½ cups chopped pecans
1 pint chocolate ice cream, softened
1 pint vanilla ice cream, softened
½ cup heavy cream
2 tablespoons confectioners' sugar
½ teaspoon vanilla
Maraschino cherry halves

Preheat oven to 375°. Cover large cooky sheet with foil; draw two 8-inch circles on foil; set aside.

In small mixing bowl beat egg white with salt at medium speed until frothy. Add ¼ cup sugar very slowly. Turn mixer to high speed and beat until stiff glossy peaks are formed. Fold in chopped nuts by hand. Divide meringue-nut mixture between two circles on foil; spread as evenly as possible to cover two circles. Bake 5-6 minutes or until meringue begins to brown; cool quickly. Carefully peel foil from meringue layers. Spread one layer with chocolate ice cream, the other with vanilla ice cream. Stack layers; freeze until firm. Just before serving, combine cream, 2 tablespoons confectioners' sugar and vanilla. Beat until soft peaks form. Mound whipped cream in center of torte; decorate with cherry halves. Cut into wedges with electric knife.

*BROILED FISH*

*OLIVE TOMATO SAUCE or CELERY GARLIC SAUCE*

*Corn on the Cob     BROILED TOMATOES*

*Shredded Cabbage and Green Pepper Salad*

*PINEAPPLE SQUARES*

*Suggested Wine: Riesling     Iced Coffee or Tea*

## BROILED FISH

1 5- to 6-pound whole salmon, snapper, bass or
  haddock, cleaned and boned
Olive Tomato Sauce or Celery Garlic Sauce (below)
1 teaspoon *each* thyme, fennel and marjoram

Brush inside of fish with half of the sauce. Tie fish securely with string. Brush outside of fish with sauce and place on greased grill. Grill fish 20-30 minutes over coals, basting continually with remaining sauce, until fish flakes easily when tested with a fork. Cut into individual servings with electric knife.

*Makes 6 servings.*

**Olive Tomato Sauce:**

2 tablespoons butter or margarine
¼ cup minced onion
⅓ cup chopped green pepper
¼ cup chopped stuffed green olives
1½ cups finely chopped peeled tomatoes
¼ teaspoon salt
1 teaspoon sugar
Dash cayenne

Melt butter or margarine in saucepan placed on one side of grill. Sauté onion and green pepper until onion is lightly browned. Add remaining ingredients; simmer 10-15 minutes or until green pepper is tender.

**Celery Garlic Sauce:**

1 cup butter or margarine
⅓ cup finely chopped celery
2 tablespoons finely chopped onions
2 cloves garlic, crushed
3 tablespoons finely chopped parsley
Salt and pepper

Melt butter or margarine in saucepan placed on one side of grill. Sauté celery, onion and garlic until tender and onion is transparent. Add remaining ingredients; simmer 10-15 minutes.

## BROILED TOMATOES

3 medium-sized tomatoes
1 tablespoon vegetable oil
1 tablespoon tarragon
Vinegar
Oregano

Grease grill. With electric knife cut tomatoes in half crosswise. Brush cut surfaces with oil; sprinkle with tarragon, vinegar and oregano; let tomatoes stand 10 minutes to absorb flavors. Arrange cut surfaces down on grill. Cook 8-10 minutes.

*Makes 6 servings.*

## PINEAPPLE SQUARES

2 cups sifted all-purpose flour
1 teaspoon baking powder
1 teaspoon salt
¼ teaspoon baking soda
1 tablespoon vanilla
½ cup shortening
1 cup firmly packed dark brown sugar
1 egg
½ cup drained crushed pineapple
1 cup white seedless raisins

Preheat oven to 375°. Grease and lightly flour two 8x8x2-inch pans. Sift flour and baking powder together. Set aside. Combine salt, soda and vanilla with shortening in mixing bowl. Gradually add sugar, mixing well after each addition until smooth. Beat in egg. Add flour mixture alternately with pineapple. Stir in raisins. Turn into prepared pans. Bake 30 minutes, or until cake springs back when lightly touched. Cool in pans 10 minutes. Remove from pans and cool on racks. Place on board and cut each cake into 16 squares with electric knife.

*Makes 32 squares.*

*LAMB SHISH KABOBS*
*RICE PILAF*
*French Bread with Melted Cheddar Cheese*
*Mixed Green Salad*   FRENCH DRESSING
*COCONUT BARS*   *Honeydew Melon with Lime Wedges*
*Suggested Wine: Chianti*   *Iced Coffee*

## LAMB SHISH KABOBS

1½ pounds boneless lamb shoulder
1 teaspoon garlic salt
¼ teaspoon freshly ground black pepper
½ teaspoon dry mustard
½ teaspoon chili powder
1 teaspoon minced onion
¼ cup cider vinegar
2 tablespoons catsup
2 tablespoons vegetable oil
15 small whole fresh mushrooms
15 small onions
15 small tomatoes or tomato wedges

With electric knife cut meat into 1½-inch cubes.° Combine garlic salt, pepper, mustard, chili powder, onion, vinegar, catsup and oil in small mixing bowl. Pour over lamb. Marinate 4-5 hours or overnight, turning three or four times. String lamb cubes on skewers alternately with mushrooms and onions. Broil over charcoal fire 15-25 minutes or until done, basting often with marinade. Turn frequently to cook evenly on all sides. String tomatoes on separate skewers and place on grill 10 minutes before end of cooking time for meat.

*Makes 6-8 servings.*

°Meat is easier to cut if partially frozen.

## RICE PILAF

2 tablespoons butter or margarine, melted
½ cup chopped onion
1 cup uncooked rice
2½ cups water
2 chicken bouillon cubes
½ cup sliced celery
½ teaspoon rosemary

Melt butter or margarine in saucepan. Sauté onion 5 minutes. Add rice and sauté until golden brown. Add remaining ingredients; cover. Cook 15 minutes over low heat or until rice is tender and liquid is absorbed.

*Makes 6-8 servings.*

## FRENCH DRESSING

1 cup vegetable oil
⅓-½ cup lemon juice
1-3 tablespoons sugar
1½ teaspoons salt
½ teaspoon paprika
½ teaspoon dry mustard
1 clove garlic

Put all ingredients in blender container; cover and run on speed 4 (or high). (Or crush garlic clove and put all ingredients in covered jar; shake well.) Chill several hours. Shake thoroughly before serving.

*Makes 1⅓-1½ cups.*

## COCONUT BARS

⅓ cup butter or margarine
1 teaspoon pumpkin pie spice
¾ cup firmly packed light brown sugar
1 large egg
1 teaspoon vanilla
⅔ cup sifted all-purpose flour
1 teaspoon baking powder
½ teaspoon salt
¾ cup moist shredded coconut

Preheat oven to 350°. Grease and lightly flour 8x8x2-inch pan. Melt butter or margarine in saucepan. Blend in pumpkin pie spice. Add sugar and mix well. Beat in egg and vanilla. Sift together flour, baking powder and salt; mix into sugar mixture. Stir in coconut. Turn into prepared pan. Bake 30 minutes. Cool in pan 10 minutes. Remove from pan. Place on board and cut into 14 bars with electric knife. Store in a tightly covered cooky jar or box.

*Makes 14 bars.*

# RECIPE INDEX